RAND NATIONAL DEFENSE RESEARCH INSTITUTE

Obtaining Life-Cycle Cost-Effective Facilities in the Department of Defense

Constantine Samaras, Abigail Haddad, Clifford A. Grammich, Katharine Watkins Webb

Prepared for the Office of the Secretary of Defense

The research described in this report was prepared for the Office of the Secretary of Defense (OSD). The research was conducted within the RAND National Defense Research Institute, a federally funded research and development center sponsored by OSD, the Joint Staff, the Unified Combatant Commands, the Navy, the Marine Corps, the defense agencies, and the defense Intelligence Community under Contract W74V8H-06-C-0002.

Library of Congress Cataloging-in-Publication Data is available for this publication.

ISBN: 978-0-8330-7935-0

Cover image: U.S. Army Corps of Engineers

Published 2013 by the RAND Corporation
1776 Main Street, P.O. Box 2138, Santa Monica, CA 90407-2138
1200 South Hayes Street, Arlington, VA 22202-5050
4570 Fifth Avenue, Suite 600, Pittsburgh, PA 15213-2665
RAND URL: http://www.rand.org/
To order RAND documents or to obtain additional information, contact
Distribution Services: Telephone: (310) 451-7002;
Fax: (310) 451-6915; Email: order@rand.org

Preface

The Department of Defense (DoD) routinely constructs, operates, and maintains a large number of facilities, such as barracks, hangars, and administrative buildings. In fiscal year (FY) 2013, DoD will spend nearly $10 billion constructing new facilities, and about the same amount or more maintaining its existing facilities. These outlays represent different components of life-cycle costs, which include those for initial construction, as well as the energy and water, operations, maintenance, repair, and replacement costs that occur over different time periods in a facility's life. By focusing on reducing the life-cycle costs of its facilities, DoD can minimize its total cost of facility ownership.

Congress has expressed concern that DoD construction methods may not obtain the most life-cycle cost-effective facilities. Consequently, it requested that DoD conduct an independent assessment of construction techniques that provide life-cycle cost-effective facilities. DoD in turn asked RAND to conduct this research to examine one aspect of this question—the process of obtaining life-cycle cost-effective facilities. This report fulfills that request.

This research was sponsored by the Office of the Deputy Under Secretary of Defense for Installations and Environment and conducted within the Acquisition and Technology Policy Center of the RAND National Defense Research Institute, a federally funded research and development center sponsored by the Secretary of Defense, the Joint Staff, the Unified Combatant Commands, the Navy, the Marine Corps, the defense agencies, and the defense Intelligence Community.

For more information on the RAND Acquisition and Technology Policy Center, see http://www.rand.org/nsrd/ndri/centers/atp.html or contact the director (contact information is provided on the web page).

Contents

Figures

Tables

Summary

The Department of Defense (DoD) routinely constructs, operates, and maintains a large number of facilities, such as barracks, hangars, and administrative buildings. In fiscal year (FY) 2013, DoD will spend nearly $10 billion constructing new facilities, and about the same amount or more operating and maintaining existing facilities. These outlays represent different components of life-cycle costs, which include those for initial construction, as well as the energy and water, operations, maintenance, repair, and replacement costs that occur over different time periods in a facility's life. By focusing on reducing the life-cycle costs of its facilities, DoD can minimize its total cost of facility ownership. Accordingly, DoD incorporates life-cycle cost-effective practices into many aspects of the military planning and construction processes.

Congress has expressed concern that DoD construction methods may not obtain the most life-cycle cost-effective facilities. Consequently, it requested that DoD conduct an independent assessment of construction techniques that provide life-cycle cost-effective facilities. The Office of the Deputy Undersecretary of Defense for Installations and Environment (ODUSD[I&E]) in turn engaged RAND to help characterize the DoD process of obtaining life-cycle cost-effective facilities.

The ODUSD(I&E) asked RAND to characterize any process issues in the programming, planning, design, budgeting, acquisition, construction operation, maintenance, or decommissioning of military construction (MILCON) projects that inhibit life-cycle cost-effective projects. This report provides RAND's description and assessment of the process used to obtain life-cycle cost-effective facilities and how that affects DoD construction options and choices. The focus of our work is the *process*, including how the incentives and barriers of various actors involved affect the overall objective of obtaining life-cycle cost-effective facilities.

Our research approach featured structured interviews with more than 30 individuals with varying roles and perspectives on the MILCON and facility sustainment processes. Altogether, we spoke with personnel from various offices within the DoD construction agent organizations who are responsible for assisting with proposed projects and executing construction, with users and maintainers of installations, and with service headquarters decisionmakers. We also spoke with private-sector construction and facilities managers. Finally, we reviewed MILCON protocols, policies, documents, and contracts to characterize the process of obtaining life-cycle cost-effective facilities.

The life cycle of a DoD facility generally consists of planning, programming, design, construction, operation, maintenance, renovation, and decommissioning. To determine the possible barriers to obtaining life-cycle cost-effective facilities, we first had to characterize the major steps in obtaining and operating DoD facilities that influence costs. We discerned eight steps in a facility's life cycle at which barriers to life-cycle cost-effectiveness might arise, shown in Figure S.1.

At each step of the MILCON process, there are different entities, roles, incentives, and barriers to obtaining life-cycle cost-effective facilities. Aligning the incentives of these various entities, and removing funding, information, timing, and resource barriers, would enable DoD to obtain facilities that are more life-cycle cost-effective.

Key Findings

DoD Is Currently Incorporating Life-Cycle Cost-Effectiveness Practices in Many Aspects of the MILCON Process

DoD, through its written design and acquisition policies and subsequent actions in the MILCON process, is currently incorporating many aspects of life-cycle cost-effectiveness into the process. We found that DoD is conducting life-cycle cost analysis when choosing from the preliminary options of new construction, existing facility renovation, or facility leasing. The outcome of this analysis, which occurs early in the

Figure S.1
Major Steps in Obtaining and Operating Department of Defense Facilities

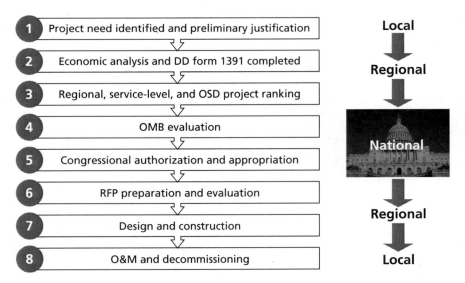

1 Project need identified and preliminary justification

2 Economic analysis and DD form 1391 completed

3 Regional, service-level, and OSD project ranking

4 OMB evaluation

5 Congressional authorization and appropriation

6 RFP preparation and evaluation

7 Design and construction

8 O&M and decommissioning

Local
Regional
National
Regional
Local

RAND RR169-S.1

MILCON process, relies on the expertise of the personnel conducting the estimate and the quality of assumptions and data used. Once an option is selected, we also found that there is clear guidance on selecting life-cycle cost-effective building systems, including energy; heating, ventilation, and air conditioning; and plumbing. Life-cycle cost decisionmaking procedures on these systems are provided by Unified Facility Criteria and Unified Facility Guide Specifications documents, and other design guidelines and performance specifications, which apply to contractors designing and constructing facilities. DoD seeks to use Energy Star products or those certified by the Department of Energy's Federal Energy Management Program in construction, which would reduce utility costs. In addition, applicable facilities are constructed to Leadership in Energy and Environmental Design (LEED) Silver facility ratings, with DoD emphasizing to contractors the importance of the energy-savings aspects of these ratings. While these actions address a critical aspect of providing life-cycle cost-effective facilities, challenges and opportunities in the process remain.

Information, Funding, and Organizational Issues Create Barriers to Life-Cycle Cost-Effectiveness for Facilities

We found that several funding and organizational barriers across the institution create challenges in obtaining life-cycle cost-effective facilities. Over the life cycle of a facility, funding is required from three primary sources. New facility design and construction funding is overwhelmingly provided by congressional authorization and appropriation of MILCON projects. Funding for facility maintenance and reinvestment is largely provided by the Sustainment, Restoration, and Modernization (SRM) accounts of the DoD budget. Facility operations funding is generally provided by Base Operations Support or other similar accounts in the DoD budget. In addition, several entities are responsible for separate phases of a facility's life cycle, each with their own incentives and measures of success that together may not align with obtaining life-cycle cost-effective facilities. Meeting mission requirements at the best value to the government through the MILCON program involves maximizing the effectiveness of capital construction expenditures, often through finding ways to provide facilities for lower initial costs. However, decisions regarding facility elements and systems made during the planning, design, and construction phase ultimately affect funding requirements for operating and maintaining facilities over the facility's 25-year or greater operating life.

Finding methods to reward actors across the different funding sources with a portion of life-cycle cost savings could incentivize a greater focus on obtaining these facilities. On a broad scale, this might involve congressional action to provide MILCON, SRM, and Base Operations Support funding in one single appropriation, with the ability to reprogram and optimize funding between these functions. On a more limited scale, Congress and DoD could analyze the life-cycle cost outcomes of the current very limited amounts of construction undertaken with SRM funding to examine if outcomes differ from MILCON programing.

Finally, aligning incentives during the operations and maintenance (O&M) phase of the facility life cycle can reduce costs. If installations are accustomed to receiving reduced O&M funding allocations, preferences toward overdesigning facilities to reduce O&M expenditures will remain. In addition, decisions regarding facility repair, renovation, and new construction are informed through existing facility quality ratings. DoD should examine the facility quality rating system to ensure that ratings are objective and verifiable and that the incentives of the actors involved are aligned with obtaining life-cycle cost-effective facilities.

Requiring Contractors to Demonstrate Life-Cycle Cost-Effectiveness in Proposals Could Raise Costs and Risks Without Guaranteeing Commensurate Savings

During our interviews and review of several MILCON request for proposal (RFP) criteria, we found that life-cycle cost criteria currently play little or no explicit role in RFP evaluation criteria, with many RFPs including initial cost as a heavily weighted evaluation factor. Since contractors will deliver proposals and projects based on DoD evaluation criteria, adding life-cycle cost-effectiveness criteria to performance specifications and proposal-evaluation criteria could potentially obtain facilities that are more life-cycle cost-effective. Yet, the challenges of incorporating nonstandard RFP evaluation criteria, such as those for life-cycle cost-effectiveness, may erode any potential benefits. Nonstandard evaluation factors require consensus on how to write the requirements and evaluation criteria for consistency and objectivity in judging proposals and enforcing results, stressing limited time and resources. A DoD pilot program to include total ownership costs is planned, which, depending on complexity and costs to evaluate, could potentially assist in reducing life-cycle costs from DoD facilities.

Despite the challenges of integrating life-cycle cost-effectiveness into the design and construction process, DoD's greater emphasis on design-build construction and performance-based specifications presents an opportunity for more-integrated design of high-performance facilities. Several other U.S. government agencies have recently experimented with integrated design-build contracts for high-performance facilities and innovative incentives for energy savings, and DoD could obtain lessons learned from these experiments. These approaches, and other methods to incentivize building commissioning and verification of energy savings, may represent design and construction contracting tools available to DoD to realize a portion of promised life-cycle savings.

Improving Standards and Performance Guidelines to Include Life-Cycle Cost-Effectiveness Elements into the Planning, Design, and Construction Processes Remains an Opportunity

DoD design guidelines drive the planning, design, and construction process for the MILCON program, and enhancing these guidelines represents an opportunity to increase DoD's ability to obtain life-cycle cost-effective facilities. This allows value engineering and life-cycle cost estimations to be performed once and diffused into designs, rather than straining design resources by performing life-cycle cost estimations for each project.

Opportunities to institutionalize life-cycle cost analysis across the services are likely to have a greater impact than simply requiring each project to undertake this resource-intensive initiative individually. This could involve data-based life-cycle cost inputs to the Unified Facilities Criteria and Unified Facility Guide Specifications, incorporating total cost of ownership data into the project development and decision-making process, and design specialization.

Construction Materials Are Largely Dictated by Building Codes Rather than the Services

In constructing buildings and choosing materials, DoD relies on the International Building Code (IBC). The IBC is a set of minimum safety standards for construction put forth and updated periodically by the International Code Council. The IBC specifies five facility construction types based on the combustibility of building materials and other elements used. Type I and Type II facilities must use noncombustible materials, such as concrete and steel, in their construction. Type III buildings must have noncombustible materials for exterior walls but may have other materials for other elements. Type IV buildings must also use noncombustible materials for their exterior walls but may use heavy timber, a type of wood construction with specific requirements in terms of materials and construction to confer fire resistance, for their other elements. Type V buildings may use combustible elements, such as wood, for both exterior and interior elements. Much of the IBC deals with safety issues, including preventing fires and minimizing the impact of any that occur. Given these goals, the IBC limits the size of buildings, both in number of stories above ground and their square feet per story, based on their building type and usage. Adoption of the IBC means that many large DoD facility designs are automatically restricted to certain building types and materials, based on size and usage requirements.

In general, average construction costs per square foot are lower for facilities constructed with combustible materials than facilities with higher levels of fire protection. It is unclear how different types of building materials compare on life-cycle costs over the broad portfolio of DoD facilities, regions, and usage patterns. There is a need for objective data across services, rather than individual case studies, to determine the life-cycle cost-effectiveness of various building materials.

Life-Cycle Cost Benchmarking Across Services and with Comparable Institutions Can Assist Decisionmaking

In this analysis, we have characterized the process that DoD uses to obtain life-cycle cost-effective facilities and identified misaligned incentives and barriers in this process. Yet, a full analysis measuring the extent to which DoD is obtaining life-cycle cost-effective facilities would require facility-level capital and O&M expenditures data over a time frame sufficient to understand and project cost trends. Using these data, an estimation of the impacts of different building designs, materials, and systems on life-cycle costs could be obtained. However, the collection, standardization, and analysis of these detailed data in the near term would be resource- and time-intensive for DoD. The potential magnitude and budgetary impact of the additional life-cycle cost savings are also unclear, given that constructing, operating, and maintaining facilities generally has represented about 2-4 percent of the DoD budget. Given this reality, in addition to the performance-based specifications and enhancements to life-cycle cost standard and guidelines discussed, an effort to benchmark DoD facility costs using existing available data could assist current decisionmaking, and DoD could incorporate new data as they become available. Benchmarking would include characterizing capital and O&M expenditures by facility type for a limited set of facilities, both within and across services, as well as against comparable institutional facility owners. This effort could potentially identify performance trends, maintenance expense "hot spots," and best practices for design and construction. Benchmarking facilities against those constructed by institutional and private-sector peers could help establish performance metrics to encourage innovation in DoD's effort to obtain life-cycle cost-effective facilities.

Acknowledgments

We thank Thadd Buzan, George Mino, and Keith Welch of ODUSD(I&E) for their thoughtful comments. We are very grateful to the service members, civilian employees, and industry professionals who were interviewed for this work, who added their unique perspectives and insights. We thank Melissa Bradley for her assistance in developing the interview protocol and Sandra Petitjean for producing the report's graphics. We are very grateful to the peer reviewers, Michael Boito and Steven M. F. Stuban, whose comments greatly improved the report. In addition, we received invaluable comments from the Office of the Secretary of Defense, Naval Facilities Engineering Command, Commander Navy Installations Command, and the United States Marine Corps. The report also benefited from helpful feedback from Cynthia Cook, Paul Deluca, Kathryn Connor, and Frank Camm.

Abbreviations

BRAC	Base Realignment and Closure
DBOM	design, build, operate, and maintain
DoD	Department of Defense
DOE	Department of Energy
FY	fiscal year
GAO	Government Accountability Office
HVAC	heating, ventilation, and air conditioning
IBC	International Building Code
LEED	Leadership in Energy and Environmental Design
MILCON	military construction
NAHB	National Association of Home Builders
NAVFAC	Naval Facilities Command
O&M	operations and maintenance
ODUSD(I&E)	Office of the Deputy Under Secretary of Defense for Installations and Environment
OMB	Office of Management and Budget
OSD	Office of the Secretary of Defense
PACES	Parametric Cost Engineering System
RFP	request for proposal
SRM	Sustainment, Restoration, and Modernization
USACE	U.S. Army Corps of Engineers

CHAPTER ONE

Introduction

The Department of Defense (DoD) manages the largest facilities portfolio in the United States, including more than 400,000 buildings and structures worth more than $620 billion (DoD, 2013). The DoD military construction (MILCON) program is the primary process for constructing new facilities for the armed services and other DoD supporting functions. In fiscal year (FY) 2013, DoD budgeted about $9.6 billion for the MILCON program.[1] DoD will spend an additional $10.2 billion maintaining and reinvesting in its existing facilities through Sustainment, Restoration, and Modernization (SRM) and Demolition funding. These amounts have varied in recent years but, combined, generally represent 2 to 4 percent of the total DoD budget (DoD, undated[a]). In addition to funding from MILCON and SRM budgets, funding from a portion of the approximately $23 billion broader Base Operations Support budget provides resources to operate facilities and provides housing services (DoD, undated[a]). Base Operations Support includes funding for purchasing electricity, natural gas, and steam used by DoD facilities, which totaled about $3.9 billion in FY 2011 (DoD, undated[a] and 2012d).

Given the funds required to construct, operate, and maintain DoD facilities, Congress has issued statutory and regulatory guidance on obtaining life-cycle cost-effective facilities. Life-cycle costs include those for initial capital, energy and water, operations, maintenance, repair, replacement, and residual value that occur over different time periods in a facility's life (Fuller, 2010). Using life-cycle cost analysis, analysts can estimate the present value of these expected future expenditures to facilitate comparison among projects on the total cost of constructing, operating, maintaining, and replacing facilities.

---

[1] Total Obligational Authority for FY2013 MILCON expenditures is $9.57 billion. This includes about $6.3 billion, $1.6 billion, and $1.7 billion for MILCON activities inside the United States, outside the United States, and in unspecified locations, respectively (DoD, undated[a]). If family housing and other programs are included, FY 2013 MILCON expenditures are about $11.2 billion.

Legislative Background on Life-Cycle Cost Analysis for Military Construction

The MILCON process is required by statute to incorporate life-cycle costing procedures.[2] 10 USC Chapter 169, Sec 2802 (c), states:

> In determining the scope of a proposed military construction project, the Secretary concerned shall submit to the President such recommendations as the Secretary considers to be appropriate regarding the incorporation and inclusion of life-cycle cost-effective practices as an element in the project documents submitted to Congress . . .

10 USC Chapter 169, Sec 2801(c)(3), defines "life-cycle cost effective" for MILCON projects as follows:

> The term 'life-cycle cost-effective,' with respect to a project, product, or measure, means that the sum of the present values of investment costs, capital costs, installation costs, energy costs, operating costs, maintenance costs, and replacement costs, as estimated for the lifetime of the project, product, or measure, does not exceed the base case (current or standard) for the practice, product, or measure.

Life-cycle cost analysis is also required in the facility decisionmaking process across the broader federal government. Executive Order 13123 requires that

> [a]gencies shall use life-cycle cost analysis in making decisions about investments in products, services, construction, and other projects to lower the Federal Government's cost and to reduce energy and water consumption.

Executive Order 13213 builds off of earlier regulatory criteria in 10 CFR 436 Subpart A, which establishes

> a methodology and procedures for estimating and comparing the life cycle costs of Federal buildings, for determining the life cycle cost effectiveness of energy con-

---

[2]   The Office of Management and Budget (OMB) offers further directives on designing life-cycle cost-effective facilities. A 2006 directive of the OMB notes that "[o]wnership costs, such as operations, maintenance (including service contracts), energy use, and disposition, can often consume more than 80 percent of the total life-cycle costs" (OMB, 2006). A 2008 OMB directive further suggests "capital programming integrat[ing] the planning, acquisition and management of capital assets into the budget decision-making process" and "to assist agencies in improving management and in complying the requirements of [t]he Energy Policy Act of 2005, Section 109, which requires that sustainable design principles are applied to the siting, design and construction of all new and replacement buildings and that new federal buildings be designed to achieve energy consumption levels that are at least 30 percent below the levels established in the 2004 International Energy Conservation Code" (OMB, 2008).

servation measures and . . . for rank ordering life cycle cost-effective measures in order to design a new Federal Building.

Among contributors to life-cycle costs for a facility are its

- external climate
- facility size and design
- usage patterns
- type of energy used
- materials and finishes
- systems for heating, cooling, lighting, and ventilation (Fuller, 2010; Fuller and Petersen, 1995; ASHRE, 2011).

Study Motivation and Research Approach

Given the importance and regulatory requirements of life-cycle cost-effective facilities, Congress requested a study assessing DoD's procedures for obtaining life-cycle cost-effective facilities. In particular, House Report 111-491 to the National Defense Authorization Act for FY 2011 expressed concerns that DoD construction methods and materials may not obtain facilities that are the most life-cycle cost-effective (U.S. House of Representatives, 2010). Accordingly, Congress asked DoD to conduct an assessment of how construction techniques and methods, contract provisions, and effective facility life assumptions affect DoD's ability to obtain life-cycle cost-effective facilities. The Office of the Deputy Under Secretary of Defense for Installations and Environment (ODUSD[I&E]) in turn engaged RAND to help characterize the DoD process of obtaining life-cycle cost-effective facilities.

The ODUSD(I&E) asked RAND to characterize any process issues in the programming, planning, design, budgeting, acquisition, construction operation, maintenance, or decommissioning of MILCON projects that inhibit life-cycle cost-effective projects. This report provides RAND's description and assessment of the process used to obtain life-cycle cost-effective facilities. The focus of our work is the *process*, including how the incentives and barriers of various actors involved affect the overall objective of obtaining life-cycle cost-effective facilities. We did not focus on evaluating specific construction techniques and methods, as these would be either explicitly or implicitly dictated through the acquisition process. Furthermore, we did not conduct a detailed analysis of the most appropriate facility life assumption, but we provide an illustrative example on how assumptions would change life-cycle cost estimates.

Our research approach featured structured interviews with more than 30 individuals with varying roles and perspectives on the MILCON and facility sustainment processes. Our interview protocol is listed in Appendix A, which provided a background for our conversations. We were able to elicit detailed opinions associated with each interviewee's areas of expertise, as well as other related topics that interviewees believed to be important for this study. Our conversations included interviews with

- DoD construction agent headquarters
- DoD construction agent field engineering offices
- DoD construction agent field contract offices
- installation public works departments
- service headquarters construction decisionmakers
- private-sector construction and facility managers.

Altogether, we spoke with personnel who are responsible for assisting with proposed projects and executing construction from the DoD construction agent organizations, the U.S. Army Corps of Engineers, the Naval Facilities Engineering Command, and the Air Force Center for Engineering and the Environment; with users of installations; and with headquarters decisionmakers. We also spoke, as noted, with private-sector construction and facilities managers. Finally, we reviewed MILCON protocols, policies, documents, and contracts, as well as other relevant life-cycle cost documents, to characterize the process of obtaining life-cycle cost-effective facilities.

We found that while DoD is incorporating some life-cycle cost elements into the MILCON process, the roles, responsibilities, and incentives of different entities in the process can pose barriers to obtaining life-cycle cost-effective facilities. Typically, for the applicable standard design, interviewees expressed that the focus is on designing to remain under the congressionally appropriated MILCON project budget, rather than life-cycle costs. Because contractors will compete to meet the expectations of those issuing requests for proposals (RFPs), the RFP process is critical to encouraging life-cycle cost-effective buildings. Yet we found that RFP design and evaluation are heavily weighted toward obtaining the lowest initial costs, rather than the lowest total or life-cycle costs. DoD may also construct buildings from many types of materials, each of which has various implications for life-cycle costs. Nevertheless, we found that material choices are sometimes dictated by building codes rather than the services.

Outline of This Report

In the next chapter, we provide an overview of the DoD facility development, construction, and operating process and barriers to life-cycle cost-effectiveness for each entity involved. In Chapter Three, we assess the role of building codes in determining construction material and how they affect life-cycle cost-effectiveness for DoD facilities. In Chapter Four, we summarize how assumptions about facility lifetimes and discount rates can influence life-cycle cost analyses. We conclude in Chapter Five with a summary of our findings and their implications.

CHAPTER TWO

The DoD Facility Development, Construction, and Operating Process and Barriers to Life-Cycle Cost-Effectiveness

The life cycle of a DoD facility generally consists of planning, programming, design, construction, operation, maintenance, renovation, and decommissioning. In this chapter, we describe the points in a facility's life cycle at which barriers to life-cycle cost-effectiveness might arise. To determine the possible barriers to obtaining life-cycle cost-effective facilities, we first characterized the major steps in obtaining and operating DoD facilities that influence costs, shown in Figure 2.1, and then examined the different entities, roles, and incentives associated with each step. We did this through our interviews and analysis of literature on the MILCON process.[1]

- The process generally begins at the local level, with installation decisionmakers identifying a project need and then preparing the preliminary justification.
- The second step is also at the local level, as those proposing the project complete the required project-specific economic analysis. The second step also includes completion of the Military Construction Project Data Sheet, DD Form 1391, requiring estimates of the construction cost, as well as a description of the proposed project.

The third, fourth, and fifth steps move from regional to service-wide to national levels:

- In the third step, regional administrators consider and rank projects from individual installations in their area, and each service's headquarters will consider and rank projects that regional administrators submit to them, which is followed by project ranking from the Office of the Secretary of Defense.
- After these assessments, a budget is submitted to OMB in the fourth step.

---

[1] References for MILCON process guidelines can be found in the bibliography. See, for example, U.S. Air Force, 2000 and 2010; U.S. Marine Corps, 2010; U.S. Navy, 2010; U.S. Army, 2009a and 2009b; USACE, 1994, 1998a, 1998b, 2005, 2008, and 2012; and DoD, 1991, 2011, 2012a, and 2012b.

Figure 2.1
Major Steps in Obtaining and Operating Department of Defense Facilities

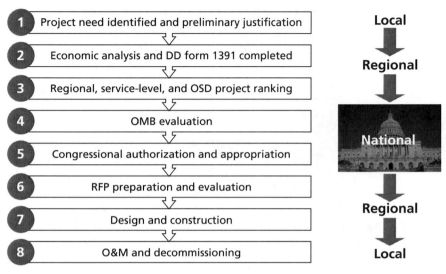

RAND *RR169-2.1*

- In the fifth step, the Office of the Secretary of Defense submits requested MILCON projects to Congress for evaluation of the proposed projects and approval of some.

Once Congress has authorized and appropriated MILCON projects and the appropriate legislation has been signed into law by the President, the process again returns to the regional and local levels.

- In the sixth step, the DoD construction agent field contract offices issue RFPs for approved projects and evaluate the competing bids.
- Following this, in the seventh step, the winning bidder works with DoD construction agent field contract offices, as well as base or installation or other local facility representatives, on design and construction of the building.
- The eighth and final step is operations and maintenance (O&M) of the constructed facility by the local installation, ending in a decision to decommission the facility at the end of its useful life, all typically done at the same local level at which the initial project need was identified.

As an example, in Appendix B we present the Navy's summary graphic of its approach to the MILCON process.

Incentives and Barriers to Life-Cycle Cost-Effectiveness at Each Step of the Military Construction Process

At each step of the MILCON process, there are different entities, roles, incentives, and barriers to obtaining life-cycle cost-effective facilities. We describe each of these below.

Step 1: Project Need Identified and Preliminary Justification

Project need may be determined either through a "top-down" or "bottom-up" process, and actors in each process have their own incentives or barriers to pursuing life-cycle cost-effective facilities. In a top-down determination, the administration, Secretary of Defense, or service headquarters may conclude that a particular capability is needed in a specific area and determine what facilities are needed to support mission requirements. Mission requirements are analyzed in the Quadrennial Defense Review, strategic and mission decisions, and other efforts. These mission requirements could be translated into facility requirements as part of the Planning, Programming, Budgeting, and Execution process (DAU, undated) or as part of the Base Realignment and Closure (BRAC) process. In a bottom-up determination, the facility need is determined locally when a facility is in need of major repair or has high operating and maintenance costs, or when local mission stakeholders require additional facilities. The installation's Department of Public Works considers, in the words of one of our interviewees, "What's available, what's the objective? Is new construction or renovation the better alternative?" The outcome of this analysis could be a MILCON project. Several interviewees noted that the top-down determination is more often used in the current environment, and local installations are mostly reacting to mission requirements, not bottom-up MILCON requests.

On the installation, the public works department and planning group conduct an independent analysis of existing assets to translate mission requirements to planning requirements. Any facility deficits that are determined are typically characterized into the additional facility area (square footage) needed to fulfill mission requirements. The planning team then preliminarily examines whether renovation of an existing facility, new construction, or leasing is more appropriate to satisfy the need. While this analysis of alternatives process is formalized in the economic analysis component in Step 2 of the MILCON process (as described in the next section), preliminary analysis is completed during the planning process to determine if moving forward is appropriate. At this initial stage in the process, the focus is on identifying options to fulfill the pressing facility need or top-down request. This may include preliminary comparisons of life-cycle cost estimates between construction, renovation, or leasing options. Consideration of minimizing life-cycle costs for each of these options at this early stage is not a primary concern, and there is limited information available to conduct such analyses. Installation user groups and mission stakeholders may be requesting a new facility in order to ameliorate an existing local deficiency or to fulfill new mission requirements.

The facility O&M expenses and obligations will be the responsibility of the installation public works department.

Service-level headquarters provide O&M funds based on square footage of facilities, usage type, and facility condition, regardless of how life-cycle cost-effective they are. Thus, headquarters are concerned with maximizing the effectiveness of maintenance funding provided to installations. Service-level headquarters balance these concerns with ensuring that mission requirements are met through the MILCON process and available capital funding. Detailed life-cycle cost analyses, if performed, are, therefore, only one component of service-level headquarters decisionmaking. (See Table 2.1.)

Step 2: Economic Analysis and DD Form 1391 Completed

After a project moves from a need to a request, a standard form is completed, DD Form 1391.[2] This form contains project information on facility type, need, size, and economic analysis; we provide a sample DD Form 1391 in Appendix C. Each DD Form 1391 ultimately serves as the funding request to Congress for that specific MILCON project. Several entities are involved in economic analysis, completion, and certification of DD Form 1391: those that complete these, whether the installations or contractors hired to complete them; DoD construction agent field engineering offices; DoD construction agent headquarters; regional service organizations; and headquarters service organizations. Installations may choose to complete DD Form 1391 themselves or may hire a contractor to do so, or it may be completed by DoD construction agent field engineering offices.

Table 2.1
Actors and Barriers to Life-Cycle Cost-Effective Facilities in the Project Need Identified and Preliminary Justification Stage

Actor	How Success Is Defined from Actor's Point of View	Barrier to Life-Cycle Cost-Effective Facilities
Installation Department of Public Works	Existing need is codified and advanced as a funding request	Need to address need for facility; life-cycle costs are not primary concern at this stage
Mission and user groups	Facilities proposed meet user requirements, timeline, and anticipated demands	MILCON, minor construction, and facility O&M performed and funded by others; do not have transparency on what is costly to maintain
Regional or headquarters service organizations	Combination of user- and service-level generated need addresses mission requirements	O&M performed by installation, who are most greatly impacted by high O&M facility costs; detailed life-cycle cost analyses sometimes not required from subordinates

---

[2]   The FY 2013 DoD budget justification data contains completed DD Form 1391 sheets for requested projects (DoD, 2012c).

We found that incentives and barriers to life-cycle cost-effectiveness at this step are most relevant to installations, who are largely responsible for completing DD Form 1391. As part of DD Form 1391 and the planning process, an economic analysis is completed for projects that exceed $2 million (USACE, 2012). The primary purpose of the economic analysis is to determine whether it is more cost-effective to keep the status quo, build a new facility, renovate an existing facility, have a combination of new construction and renovation, or lease a facility from another entity (Smigel, 2010). We found that installation planners perform life-cycle cost analysis across these options when conducting the economic analysis, as part of the DD Form 1391 preparation. Interviewees told us that installations primarily use the ECONPACK software package to complete economic analyses.[3] There are several types of economic analyses that could be performed as part of DD Form 1391. A full mission requirement economic analysis is performed when there is more than one viable alternative to satisfy the project need. In a full mission requirement economic analysis, as stated by one interviewee, "you engage in full life-cycle cost analysis for each alternative to identify which would be most cost-effective." The full mission requirements economic analysis consists of

- preparing assumptions
- estimating initial and O&M expenses and residual values for all alternatives
- documenting sources and derivations
- documenting nonmonetary considerations
- preparing cost sensitivity analyses
- obtaining net present values from the ECONPACK software
- preparing results and recommendations, as well as additional language for updating previously submitted analyses, if applicable.

A partial mission requirements economic analysis is performed for an identified need with only one viable course of action (such as new construction). Installations conducting partial missions requirements economic analysis do not conduct detailed cost analyses; instead, they justify the project based on the nonmonetary barriers of the other options, such as physical space or regulatory constraints (Smigel, 2010). Another analysis type is a nominal missions requirements economic analysis, which is limited to projects explicitly exempted from a detailed analysis by law, such as chemical weapons demilitarization projects (Smigel, 2010). The final type of economic analysis is a return on investment analysis, which is associated with meeting an existing requirement at lower cost rather than fulfilling new mission requirements. An example would be a mix of renovation and new construction to repurpose an existing warehouse as an in-processing center, which would replace an existing in-processing center with higher costs (Smigel, 2010). Planners performing a return on investment economic analysis

---

[3] The ECONPACK software is described at USACE, undated(b).

would perform calculations similar to a full missions requirements economic analysis and also estimate savings-to-investment ratios, discounted payback periods, and return on investment (Smigel, 2010).

An interviewee added that the result of the economic analysis "[is] written to educate the decisionmaker, but it doesn't make the decision." Nonmonetary and mission considerations are also inputs to facility decisionmaking. Another interviewee told us that once it is determined that new construction is the most viable option,

> not much life-cycle cost analysis takes place within the new construction option. There are minimal project details at this stage, and you are really not doing life-cycle cost analysis, but conducting an economic analysis for project justification among options to fulfill a project need. As a result, a ceiling number for costs per square foot are determined, which pretty much locks in initial construction costs without a lot of flexibility down the road.

If new construction is determined to be the most viable option, installation planners use the DoD Facilities Pricing Guide and the Programming Cost Estimates for Military Construction guidelines (UFC 3-701-01 and UFC 3-730-01, contained in DoD, 2012a) for preparation of the DD Form 1391 construction estimates. The Facilities Pricing Guide, which is updated annually, provides estimates of military facility unit costs (dollars/square foot) by facility type for U.S. facilities based on actual costs of projects awarded by the services in the previous five years. Planners use the Facilities Pricing Guide costs for initial cost estimating purposes. However, several interviewees expressed the difficulties of programming cost estimates using five-year historical average costs. They noted that changes in the overall economy affect the prices of MILCON projects. During periods of high economic activity, previously programmed costs will be below actual prices of materials and services, forcing installations to reduce the scope of in-progress projects to remain under the programmed amount. Conversely, during the recent economic downturn, historical average prices were higher than current in-progress projects, allowing installations to include many enhancements and improvements while remaining under the programmed amounts.

Installations often conduct more-detailed, customizable parametric cost estimates during the DD Form 1391 stage. While the facility design is very preliminary at this stage in the process (generally considered by interviewees to be about 5–15 percent complete), a parametric estimate allows for the cost of detailed and specific building elements (e.g., a metal roof or specific mechanical system) to be considered. These elements often act as cost "placeholders" as one interviewee told us, and while detailed life-cycle cost analysis is done during the design phase, having these elements included in DD Form 1391 provides the funds necessary for their eventual inclusion. The value of parametric estimating depends on the quality of the input assumptions and on a defined project scope (DoD, 2012a). As of June 2011, the only approved parametric estimating software is the Parametric Cost Engineering System (PACES),[4] and training is required before it can be used (DoD, 2012a).

Installation departments of public works are heavily involved with generating the DD Form 1391 and are ultimately responsible for maintaining constructed facilities. We hypothesized that those at the installation will want life-cycle cost-effective buildings because, ultimately, they will have responsibility for maintaining them—and having life-cycle cost-effective buildings would help them stretch their O&M funding further. Ideally, these incentives would lead installation departments of public works to seek the most life-cycle cost-effective facilities during the economic analysis and DD Form 1391 stage of the project. The responses from interviewees verified this hypothesis in principle but cited several barriers that prevent full realization. Committing additional analysis for each DD Form 1391 to analyze or refine life-cycle cost estimates must be balanced with available resources. One interviewee told us,

> Until the DD Form 1391 is approved by Congress, there isn't any MILCON money to spend. Everything [regarding DD Form 1391 development and design] up until that point is [funded by] operations and maintenance. This is the same money used to pay the electrical bill, and they are frugal with that money. Money and time constraints keep us from doing more up-front analysis.

Interviewees told us that, generally, 5 to 15 percent of the total design effort for a facility is completed during the DD Form 1391 process, and judgment is required to perform a facility construction cost estimate with only preliminary design details. One interviewee said, "Previously we were designing to 35 percent complete in the DD Form 1391 process, which added detail but also substantial costs." Additionally, another interviewee told us that obtaining a facility to serve a need is a priority, and that, "logically, you want the best building . . . but sometimes budget comes into play." As other interviewees said, installation personnel may not have enough design information or funding available to provide detailed life-cycle cost estimates when completing DD Form 1391. The lack of time and resources available, coupled with the low probability of funding for any given project, means that installations are not likely to find spending money on a life-cycle cost estimate on any given project to be worthwhile, interviewees told us. Some available software for estimating life-cycle costs may allow installations (or, possibly, others preparing DD Form 1391s or economic analyses for them) to include such costs in their analyses.[5] Such software, one interviewee said, "is fairly easy [to use] if you have the data. [But] that's sometimes complex at the local

---

[4]   PACES is available at Whole Building Design Guide, 2012b.

[5]   See Appendix F of UFC 3-740-05 (DOD, 2012a). For example, several software tools have been developed by the Army to assist in DD 1391 generation and economic analysis (USACE, undated[a]). The Navy produced a 1391 Sustainable Design Cost Tool (Naval Facilities Engineering Command, undated). The Department of Energy (DOE) produced the Building Life-Cycle Cost Programs (DOE, 2012b).

level." Public works maintenance software is generally contained in a separate system from planning and design tools. Additionally, differences in culture between maintenance personnel and planning and design personnel were also cited as a barrier to integrated project development.

One interviewee notes, "There isn't really a process for analyzing life-cycle costs. There's been a push to move the life-cycle cost analysis earlier in the process, but we're not sure how meaningful this is going to be. The only way to do life-cycle cost analysis is during design, and at that point the funding has already been authorized and appropriated by Congress." Another suggests using MILCON money to analyze life-cycle costs in early project stages: "In ideal situations, we'd get upfront military construction money to make better decisions. But we don't have money to do that. Right now, we look hard, push [public works departments] as hard as we can. Sometimes we're lucky and get to put things in a project we might not always get to do. Sometimes we have to leave things out. Money and time constraints keep us from doing more upfront analysis." Another interviewee countered this view by stating that there is some limited MILCON planning and design funding available, typically up to a year before congressional approval of projects. Because of the multiyear project development cycle, this planning and design funding is likely only to refine late-stage project proposals.

For most projects, a planning charrette is undertaken, which is a meeting that brings together stakeholders to define project requirements, options, and costs in concert with the installation overall planning efforts. These charrettes are generally funded with installation O&M funding, so the same trade-offs apply to maximizing the use of scarce O&M resources on project planning and life-cycle cost estimates. One interviewee suggested that if an installation chooses to fund a planning charrette, "external supplemental funding should be provided to undertake analysis of options for life-cycle cost-effective buildings." A life-cycle cost analysis during a planning charrette could involve engineering and maintenance offices to integrate building design, systems, and elements into decisionmaking to maximize life-cycle cost-effectiveness.

Designing facilities to receive Leadership in Energy and Environmental Design (LEED; U.S. Green Building Council, 2012) certification codifies some aspects of life-cycle cost considerations, if annual utility and other expenses are substantially reduced relative to any cost premiums associated with achieving certification. The National Defense Authorization Act for FY 2012 requires installations to seek a waiver from the Secretary of Defense to spend resources to achieve the two highest LEED certifications (Platinum or Gold), which can help in obtaining facilities with higher levels of water and energy efficiency, among other environmental characteristics. Currently, most applicable facilities are designed to achieve LEED Silver status.

Garrison or installation commanders also are involved in the DD Form 1391 process, as they sign and approve each DD Form 1391. Each commander benefits and improves his or her installation by receiving MILCON funding, so his or her incentives are to facilitate this process. It is also likely this commander will not be stationed at this particular installation during the O&M phase of the facility's life cycle, which incentivizes him or her to focus more on initial capital construction than on life-cycle costs. Installations and the services also consider nonmonetary issues, such as user convenience and quality of life, when proposing facilities. Finally, given the intense competition for project funding, some interviewees told us that installations may seek to minimize initial costs, regardless of their relationship to ultimate life-cycle costs, so as to increase the likelihood of project funding. However, other interviewees disagreed with this rationale.

The DoD construction agent field offices are responsible for assisting installations with the completion and initial certification of DD Form 1391. One interviewee expressed concern that requiring additional life-cycle cost analysis by installations would greatly increase staffing needs at installations and noted that the number of planners at installations had dropped considerably over the past several years. This interviewee expressed the difficulties of preparing and reviewing current DD Form 1391s and expressed hesitation regarding making the process more complex.

A larger process question is the effectiveness of DD Form 1391 itself in encouraging life-cycle cost-effectiveness. Some interviewees suggested modernizing the form and requiring a life-cycle cost analysis for at least some portions of proposed projects. If detailed O&M data by facility type were available, assembled, and reliable, an estimate of annualized life-cycle costs for the project broken down by major cost categories would, ideally, be a component of DD Form 1391. (See Table 2.2.)

Table 2.2
Actors and Barriers to Life-Cycle Cost-Effective Facilities in the Economic Analysis and DD Form 1391 Stage

Actor	How Success Is Defined from Actor's Point of View	Barrier to Life-Cycle Cost-Effective Facilities
Installation Department of Public Works	Completed DD Form 1391s are advanced toward consideration for funding	Do not have funding, staff, and time resources to conduct additional appropriate life-cycle cost analysis during DD Form 1391 development
Installation or garrison commander	Completed DD Form 1391s are advanced toward consideration for funding. Also, commander may desire increased capital spending occurring on installation	Likely to have moved to a different post when facility O&M costs are realized
DoD construction agent field engineering office	DD Form 1391s submitted meet consistency and quality requirements	Limited incentives to propose or recommend initial cost estimates below or above those of Unified Facility Pricing Guidelines
DoD construction agent headquarters	DD Form 1391s submitted by installation meet consistency and quality requirements	Limited incentives to propose or recommend initial cost estimates below or above those of Unified Facility Pricing Guidelines

Step 3: Regional, Service-Level, and OSD Project Ranking

In the third step of the MILCON process, regional and service-wide organizations meet to rank projects by importance for the region or across the service. On a regional level, the Assistant Chief of Staff for Installation Management, Mission Communications and Operations Maintenance personnel, major commands, and specialized commands, such as the Army Training and Doctrine Command or Forces Command, meet to rank projects that installations submit by importance for their region. The services in turn use these regional priorities to determine the service-wide priorities for projects, which are then evaluated and ranked by the Office of the Secretary of Defense. One interviewee noted that at the project ranking stage, "projects are assumed to be economically valid and justified through the DD Form 1391 process."

Regional and service-wide organizations face barriers to pursuing life-cycle cost-effective projects. First, they may submit many more funding requests than will eventually be funded, both because of mission requirements and, as several interviewees told us, "so as to highlight project need and increase the likelihood of core project funding." In proposing more projects, the regional organizations and the services, like the individual installations, are less likely to research life-cycle cost-effectiveness for any given project. Second—like the individual installations—the regions, service headquarters, and the Office of the Secretary of Defense, seeking to have the greatest possible number of funded projects, may minimize initial costs for these projects. As noted earlier, minimizing initial costs may conflict with minimizing overall life-cycle costs, especially if minimizing overall life-cycle costs were to require a larger initial investment in constructing a facility. Third, the forms and exhibits under evaluation generally do not include O&M or life-cycle cost estimates. Time constraints are an additional barrier for the ranking process, as DoD construction agents are managing multiple timelines, and the project list is dynamic.

Those evaluating projects may have still other considerations. One interviewee noted that project ranking is conducted with multi-criteria objectives, with cost being just one factor. This was validated by a second interviewee who suggested that prioritization of projects can change as project sponsors add their own reviews to those of regional planners. (See Table 2.3.)

Step 4: OMB Evaluation

The joint review of the DoD budget by OMB and the Office of the Secretary of Defense (OSD) occurs between September and December before the beginning of the fiscal year (DiStasio, 2011). For example, the joint review for FY 2012, which began in October 2011, occurred between September and December of 2010.

The joint review focuses on the administration's priorities, as well as such general areas as "program phasing and pricing, compliance with DoD funding policies, and efficient execution of funds, based on performance metrics" (DAU, undated). As part of this process, OSD and OMB hold budget meetings to gather information on

Table 2.3
Actors and Barriers to Life-Cycle Cost-Effective Facilities in the Regional, Service-Level, and OSD Project Ranking Stage

Actor	How Success Is Defined from Actor's Point of View	Barrier to Life-Cycle Cost-Effective Facilities
DoD construction agent headquarters	Highest-ranked projects meet the most urgent local need	Proposed project list is dynamic, and decisions are delayed; managing multiple timelines under time constraints
Regional service organization	Mission requirements likely to be satisfied by list of proposed projects; capital construction is maximized for each region	Many more projects submitted than eventually will be funded; approves projects if they are consistent with DoD facility pricing guidelines
Service headquarters	Mission requirements likely to be satisfied by list of proposed projects; capital construction is maximized for each service; programming the most mission capabilities with the limited MILCON funds available	No established link between MILCON funding and O&M on DD Form 1391; view is that economic validity of project is already established by DD Form 1391. Mission need takes precedence over life-cycle cost considerations.
Office of the Secretary of Defense	Mission requirements likely to be satisfied by list of proposed projects. Projects submitted fit within goals of administration's budget and priorities	Need to maximize number of projects and have limited total budget leads to relying on projects with lower initial costs; list of projects considered is dynamic

budget justifications from component and OSD staff. They then issue program budget decisions. At the end of this process, the Secretary of Defense may meet with the President to settle any major differences between what DoD wants and what OMB has approved. After budget decisions are finalized, the DoD comptroller prepares the President's budget for submission to Congress (Adams, 2008).

In OMB evaluation, the OMB reviews the DD Form 1391 submissions for projects proposed by OSD. Interviewees told us that for some projects, OMB may recommend a percentage cut in proposed funding. This is to bring proposed costs in line with what OMB believes historical estimates indicate.

In this evaluation, there are two barriers to life-cycle cost-effectiveness. First, OMB compares proposed project costs with actual average costs realized by the services in the previous five years. As discussed above in Step 2, these historical costs fluctuate with the overall economy, and actual costs realized by projects are higher than historical costs realized during economic downturns. An interviewee told us that "many of the sustainable energy and life-cycle cost-effective systems that we would like to include often have a hard time getting in because OMB says that this type of facility has historically been constructed cheaper." Another interviewee told us that with a detailed parametric cost estimate included in DD Form 1391, OMB will approve advanced systems and nonstandard construction, but this requires expertise and resources by the team completing the form. Second, OMB is only evaluating project initial costs. If these projects were designed to minimize initial costs rather than to reduce life-cycle costs, then OMB would be comparing proposed projects to a standard that minimizes initial costs rather than reduces life-cycle costs. (See Table 2.4.)

Step 5: Congressional Evaluation and Approval

Three entities have primary roles in congressional evaluation and approval (in addition, of course, to members of Congress who ultimately vote on funding projects). First, DoD reviews final cost estimates and submits a budget justification to Congress.[6] Second, the Congressional Armed Services Committees approve and authorize a number of projects on which the whole Congress votes. Third, the congressional appropriations committees allocate funding levels for a number of projects on which the whole Congress also votes. Finally, the appropriate legislation is passed by both the House and Senate and signed by the President into law.[7]

There are two primary barriers to pursuing life-cycle cost-effectiveness in the congressional evaluation and approval process. First, the congressional committees are only evaluating initial costs, so as to minimize costs to the government and taxpayers during a specific authorization and appropriation cycle. Second, the appropriations committees determine O&M funding separately from construction funding. As a result, OSD and the services have only limited ability to increase construction funding in such a way that it could later reduce O&M funding through constructing buildings that incorporate life-cycle cost-effectiveness.

The end result, as one of our interviewees told us, is a "ceiling" for the project that ultimately determines how much flexibility there will be in construction for life-cycle cost-effective features. As this interviewee said, "We can escalate or reprogram a little. But [what is] enacted by Congress is what we have to work with."

Interviewees stated that their goal is to have RFPs for projects ready to advertise to the contracting community in the first quarter of the fiscal year in which they are authorized and appropriated. One interviewee expressed that delays in congressional

Table 2.4
Actors and Barriers to Life-Cycle Cost-Effective Facilities in the OMB Evaluation Stage

Actor	How Success Is Defined from Actor's Point of View	Barrier to Life-Cycle Cost-Effective Facilities
Office of the Secretary of Defense	Slate of proposed projects is approved and submitted to Congress	Incentives to have low initial costs to be consistent with historical costs
OMB	Capital costs of proposed projects are consistent with historical costs	Evaluating projects based on initial costs

---

[6]   For the FY 2013 DoD budget justification data submitted to Congress, see DoD, 2012c.

[7]   For a listing of MILCON-related legislation, see DoD (undated[b]).

authorization and appropriation reduce the time available to prepare, advertise, and evaluate RFPs. (See Table 2.5.)

Step 6: Request for Proposal Preparation and Evaluation

DoD construction agent field engineering and contract offices, installations, contractors, and evaluation committees all have roles in the RFP process. DoD construction agent field engineering offices and contract offices are responsible for preparing, advertising, evaluating, and awarding design and construction contracts. They, with input from installations, create the requirements, such as mechanical requirements for plumbing systems or for heating, ventilation, and air conditioning (HVAC) systems, that are listed in the RFPs and based on Unified Facilities Criteria. Contractors submit proposals based on the requirements and evaluation factors. Evaluation committees, which may have membership from the installation, the military district, and facility users, including commands (such as the Army Training and Doctrine Command), review and award proposals. One interviewee observed that "the evaluation committees generally only have one person representing the interests of O&M costs for an installation [with the balance of the committee interested in initial costs and other factors]."

As we describe in Table 2.6, there are two primary contracting approaches of design and construction delivery for the MILCON program: (1) design, bid, build and (2) design-build. The choice between these delivery methods affects the type and evaluation of RFPs, which are led by DoD construction agents. Under a design, bid, build approach, DoD first awards a design contract to an architectural/engineering contractor to produce detailed facility design drawings and specifications. Alternatively, sometimes the designs are completed in house by the DoD construction agents. With these completed drawings as a basis, the DoD construction agents then compete and award a separate contract to a construction firm to construct the facility. Under a design-build approach, a single contract is awarded to a contractor who is responsible for both designing and constructing the facility (California Legislative

Table 2.5
Actors and Barriers to Life-Cycle Cost-Effective Facilities in the Congressional Authorization and Appropriation Stage

Actor	How Success Is Defined from Actor's Point of View	Barrier to Life-Cycle Cost-Effective Facilities
Office of the Secretary of Defense	Slate of proposed projects is authorized and appropriated	Incentives to have low initial costs to get as many projects as possible included
Congress	Slate of proposed projects meet mission and cost criteria within proposed budget; maximize construction and economic benefits to constituents	Evaluates MILCON and O&M expenses separately. Delays in authorization and appropriation reduce the time available for proposal evaluation

Table 2.6
The Two Primary Approaches of Design and Construction Delivery for the MILCON Program

Approach	Responsibility for Design	Responsibility for Construction
Design, bid, build	Completed either in house by DoD construction agent or by architectural/ engineering contractor responding to RFP for design	Construction contractor responding to RFP for construction contract for a completed design
Design-build	Single contractor responds to one RFP for design and construction contract	

SOURCE: Adapted from California Legislative Analyst's Office, 2005.

Analyst's Office, 2005). The DoD construction agent field engineering and contract offices, through the design-build RFP, detail the minimum performance specifications required for the specific facility, and the construction firm commences the project. There are advantages and disadvantages to each construction delivery approach with respect to costs, timing, quality, and control.[8] Our interviewees told us that they could choose which approach to use, but "there has been a constant trend toward more design-build MILCON projects over the past several years, accounting for greater than 60 percent of projects." Interviewees cited greater time and cost savings as the dominant drivers of the trend toward design-build construction. The Marine Corps has also recently experimented with an extension of the design-build approach: a design, build, operate, and maintain (DBOM) agreement for a wastewater treatment facility at Camp Pendleton (CDM Smith, 2012). A DBOM approach would integrate life-cycle maintenance and costs into project design and construction and could potentially provide lower life-cycle costs to DoD, depending on the negotiated price and quality terms of the DBOM service agreement. DoD can examine the Camp Pendleton DBOM experience for lessons learned and for future consideration of the DBOM approach for large infrastructure assets.

The RFP process is one of several critical junctures in the MILCON process during which life-cycle cost-effectiveness could potentially be promoted. The DoD construction agent field offices establish the metrics for evaluating proposals. Several sections of RFPs have been standardized by facility and region and are customizable with online tools and templates.[9] Contractors will deliver proposals and projects based on DoD evaluation criteria. Currently, the primary evaluation criteria for construction proposals are generally cost or price, past contractor performance, contractor technical or mission capabilities, and risk. The Naval Facilities Command (NAVFAC) uses different evaluation criteria, including cost or price, past performance, technical

---

[8]   For further discussion on the advantages and disadvantages of these construction delivery approaches, see, for example, reports by the California Legislative Analyst's Office (2005) and the GAO (1997).

[9]   See, for example, USACE RFP Wizard, undated, and Whole Building Design Guide, 2012a.

approach, experience, safety, technical solution, energy and sustainable design, and small business status.

We learned that life-cycle costs are now typically a small part of proposal-evaluation criteria, if they are included at all. Several interviewees said that they could not remember any specific instance of life-cycle cost-effectiveness explicitly detailed in an RFP. Other interviewees noted that some RFPs include elements of life-cycle cost analysis in their criteria, but these are often included as subelements in other primary criteria. For example, systems costs may be among the "energy and sustainable design" criteria, while maintenance costs may be among the "technical and performance" criteria. All nonprice criteria—that is, all criteria not related to the initial price of constructing the facility—may be prioritized in the RFP evaluation factors as more important, equally important, or less important than the cost or price. Contractors responding to RFPs are less likely to incorporate features promoting life-cycle cost-effectiveness in construction on proposals in which life-cycle cost-effectiveness criteria are combined with all nonprice criteria, and especially those in which all nonprice criteria are deemed less important than cost or price. Interviewees told us that as RFPs trend more toward the design-build approach, however, many RFP technical evaluation criteria are weighted more importantly than price. But several interviewees were concerned about how to evaluate life-cycle cost-effective design proposals for design-build contracts in which "the full design hasn't been developed yet."

Installations can help determine the importance of different proposal-evaluation criteria and, in particular, help promote life-cycle cost-effectiveness in proposals. Interviewees described the proposal language and evaluation to be requirements-based and generally not prescribing specific building materials or methods. "If a contractor proposes to use prefabricated, wood-framed, or [some] other construction method that could potentially be less expensive, then it would get full consideration as long as it meets the requirements," one interviewee said. Interviewees told us that if installations emphasize reducing life-cycle costs for the facility, then proposal-evaluation criteria are likely to include measures of life-cycle cost-effectiveness. Installations may also, in setting evaluation criteria, define a willingness to trade among initial price, schedule, life-cycle costs, and other considerations. Nevertheless, in the current budgetary environment, nearly all installations prioritize initial price in their proposal-evaluation criteria, according to interviewees.

However, many interviewees expressed that requiring contractors to include life-cycle cost-effectiveness estimates into RFP responses would subject DoD to additional risk without guaranteeing commensurate benefits. If installations seek to emphasize life-cycle cost-effectiveness in proposal-evaluation criteria, they may face information, capability, resource, and timing barriers for including those. Nonstandard evaluation criteria, such as those for life-cycle costs, require additional expertise, time, and resources that DoD construction agent field offices and installations may not have. One interviewee noted that, for a recent RFP that included nonstandard sustainability evaluation criteria, they had to "reach throughout the entire organization to pull together the expertise to get it completed." Nonstandard evaluation factors require consensus on how to write the requirements and evaluation criteria for consistency and objectivity in judging proposals, further stressing time and resources. An interviewee told us that "we have to be very conscious of [selection criteria]. We've selected the contractor based on rules. These rules need to be objective and verifiable. We have to comply [with] every part of the RFP requirement." Another challenge with requiring contractors to demonstrate life-cycle cost-effectiveness on proposals is the short time frames involved. In the limited time between RFP advertisement and due date (generally eight weeks), contractors would be required to develop justification for life-cycle cost elements of their proposed approach, either with their own internal proposal funding or through a qualified stipend from DoD. One interviewee said that in this time frame, "upfront decisions would be made that aren't necessarily cheap or fully researched, and we'll probably receive higher bids." It is also "unclear the government would receive several credible bidders if extended at-risk life-cycle cost analysis is required in the RFP."

The timing of congressional MILCON authorizations and appropriations can also greatly affect the ability of installations to include life-cycle costs and other non-standard criteria in their RFPs. Ideally, congressional authorization and appropriation for MILCON plans would be made one year prior to the start of the new fiscal year. In recent years, however, authorizations have been made later in the preceding fiscal year. As a result, there is a shorter window in which to issue RFPs and make awards, with RFPs often not even issued until the third quarter of the preceding fiscal year. As a result, interviewees told us, it is increasingly difficult to incorporate nonstandard evaluation criteria, such as those for life-cycle cost-effectiveness. Interviewees were also very concerned with the prospect of verifying and enforcing contractor life-cycle cost savings claims made during the proposal process, noting that if DoD identifies promised savings that then fail to materialize several years after the facility is in operation, there are limited mechanisms to recover damages from contractors. Follow-up to determine whether buildings met stated life-cycle costs and to enforce any deviations requires additional DoD time and resources. A DoD pilot program to include total ownership costs is planned, which, depending on its complexity and evaluation costs, could potentially assist in reducing life-cycle costs from DoD facilities.

Because installations want to stretch their O&M dollars, they have an incentive to issue requirements that will support life-cycle cost-effective buildings. At the same time, because installations do not directly benefit from project bid savings, installations do not have all the incentives they might otherwise have to require value engineering and life-cycle cost-effective buildings. They also have to satisfy users who may have facility priorities other than life-cycle cost-effectiveness.

Nevertheless, DoD attempts to satisfy statutory and regulatory requirements for life-cycle cost-effectiveness in several ways. Design criteria for new facilities require the chosen products and systems to be competitive in life-cycle costs (see, for example,

NAVFAC, 2012; Stumpf et al., 2011). RFPs, through the specifications in the Unified Facilities Criteria, also specify use of products and systems designed to minimize utility costs. Projects also pursue LEED Silver ratings where applicable, although, as noted earlier, pursuing Gold or Platinum ratings requires a waiver. Finally, DoD seeks to use Energy Star products or those certified by the DOE's Federal Energy Management Program in construction. (See Table 2.7.)

Step 7: Design and Construction

The DoD construction agent field contract and engineering offices, designers, contractors, and installation user groups have roles in the design and construction process. DoD construction agent field contract and engineering offices oversee contractors, who in turn build the facility. As noted, for design-build projects, contractors may also design the facility; design and construction, when both contracted, may be done by the same or different subcontractors. DoD construction agent field engineering offices manage design when design is done internally. Whether a contractor both designs and builds a facility or designs it for another entity to build can affect construction techniques and consideration of life-cycle costs. One interviewee told us that contractors who both design and build are required to look at life-cycle costs, while those who conduct only design follow Unified Facility Criteria and service criteria to ensure that the facility stays within the contract price.

Designers have both incentives for and barriers to pursuing life-cycle cost-effective facilities. Because project cost estimates are based on historical cost estimates, as discussed previously, in periods of economic downturns and lower costs, designers may be able to use higher initial cost estimates, based on historical cost estimates that are higher than current prices. As one of our interviewees explained, "Historical costs are

Table 2.7
Actors and Barriers to Life-Cycle Cost-Effective Facilities in the RFP Preparation and Evaluation Stage

Actor	How Success Is Defined from Actor's Point of View	Barrier to Life-Cycle Cost-Effective Facilities
DoD construction agent field contract office	RFP is prepared, advertised, evaluated, and awarded on schedule	Life-cycle costs are rarely considered as part of evaluation factors for contractor
DoD construction agent field engineering offices	RFP is prepared, advertised, evaluated, and awarded on schedule	May not have time or resources to include life-cycle cost considerations into RFP; lack of life-cycle cost criteria and standards
Contractors responding to RFP	Awarded competitive contract	Will propose to performance standards viewed necessary to win
Installation	RFP is awarded on schedule	Typically do not emphasize life-cycle cost-effectiveness as important for RFP evaluation criteria

based on previous costs, so changes in the economy have a huge impact on whether a project is affordable or we have to alter it." The services may occupy structures in their original intended use for periods of 30 years or more, which often affects facility design choices. One interviewee told us, "My experience in private sector is that construction methods are not equal in private sector as in government. A private store may only plan on being in their building for 15–20 years." Another interviewee said, "In comparing between the private sector and the services, you need to look at someone who intends to be in the building for 50–60 years. This includes the federal government or a university. Those entities are the same as us; we intend to use these buildings for a long time." Another interviewee qualified this view and believed that the appropriate building life assumption should be determined on a case-by-case basis and sometimes should be shorter as missions and technologies change. The interviewee cited that World War II hangars were designed to house large aircraft, but these are now used to house much smaller planes, adding, "I don't think we should always assume a 50-year life cycle." Similarly, the evolving standards for unaccompanied personnel housing demonstrate the need to design for adaptability to new requirements. Pre–World War II unaccompanied personnel housing was constructed to be durable, and rooms typically housed multiple people sharing a common bathroom. In the 1980s and 1990s, Army unaccompanied personnel housing consisted of two connected rooms, with two people in each room, sharing a common bathroom. Starting in 2005, the Army standards provided for two private rooms, sharing a bathroom and kitchenette, with standards continuing to evolve toward apartment-style housing (Neuhaus et al., 2010). Thus, designing for longevity can in some cases lock in previous standards for infrastructure investments, as mission requirements change. The need to design for adaptability, while minimizing life-cycle costs, remains an important consideration for the actors in the DoD facility development cycle to consider.

Often, facilities may be of a standard design. As one interviewee told us, designs can be for the "same building type wherever. So, barracks at one fort, same [at] another . . . . [S]tandard designs specify what is to be constructed. So, an inherent assumption is that some engineer somewhere has gone through and figured out that this design is the most effective way to satisfy it."

Changes during the building process, including those to incorporate more life-cycle cost-effective features, can be difficult to accommodate. As one interviewee told us, "We can't get the full value from design-build as a private building [can]. We have to go through the whole modification process, which is long." Another interviewee spoke of a prevailing attitude from DoD that design and construction should focus on reducing initial costs, rather than worry about life-cycle costs.

Sometimes, designers may have to address conflicting goals. One interviewee told us of balancing contract enhancements with potential life-cycle costs with installation user groups during the design and construction phases, saying, "I have recommended [life-cycle cost-effective building] finishes to installation folks. And they say, 'I need as much square footage as I can get versus, say, a brick finish.' Because the funding is separate—the maintenance costs comes from users. They'll say, 'No, I want more space [instead of better finishes], I want my people to be comfortable.'" One interviewee offered examples of installations overdesigning a facility to reduce O&M costs while increasing initial capital costs. The interviewee said, "Since [DoD facility O&M] is always underfunded,[10] installations often demand overdesigned facilities that have the lowest O&M costs, even if they are not life-cycle cost-effective."

Those designing and constructing MILCON facilities face constraints not prevalent in the private sector. These requirements may conflict with life-cycle cost-effectiveness both by driving up construction costs and by mandating particular building features that increase O&M costs. As one interviewee told us, "One of the problems I've always had [is the] trade-off between energy efficiency and antiterrorism standards." The Government Accountability Office (GAO) (2010) identified conflicts between antiterrorism construction standards and sustainable design goals, particularly those related to building density. Meeting antiterrorism standards tends to reduce the density of developments, while meeting sustainable design goals tends to increase the density of developments. Nevertheless, the services reported being able to meet both sets of goals (GAO, 2010).

Still other requirements can potentially increase construction costs, according to interviewees. These requirements include those for base access, payment of prevailing wages, tighter enforcement of construction-safety regulations, "buy American" regulations, site-specific cultural or archeological sensitivities, and other issues. Such increases to construction costs leave less room below the ceiling that Congress may set for a project to include life-cycle cost-effective features. One interviewee wondered if DoD used overly conservative fire protection design criteria, which, if true, would increase costs relative to following standard fire codes. Deviating from the current level of fire protection to reduce life-cycle costs would only be prudent if overall casualty risk from fires did not increase. As discussed in the next section, design choice could also be influenced by the role of property insurance and potential risk of minor and major damages. Appropriate fire protection design criteria for DoD facilities remain an important area of future research.

One additional challenge in decisionmaking for designers regarding life-cycle cost-effectiveness is the variation in building element costs for different facility types. Appendix C of the Programming Cost Estimates for Military Construction Guidelines (DoD, 2012a) lists the percentage of total initial facility costs comprised by major building elements. For example, the building's superstructure is the most expensive element of a general administrative facility, at about 18 percent of the total initial cost, while interior finishes make up about 10 percent. Conversely, for enlisted barracks, interior finishes make up about 19 percent, while building superstructure is about

---

[10] See, for example, GAO (2008).

13 percent. For other facilities, HVAC represents the most expensive building element (DoD, 2012a). Hence, designers may spend their limited time and resources conducting life-cycle cost analysis for systems that represent various proportions of project initial costs across different facility types. The life-cycle cost savings associated with these depend on assumptions on maintenance costs savings, replacement schedules, utility prices, escalation, usage, and other factors, which further add to the complexity and lack of information available during the facility design process.

Despite the challenges of integrating life-cycle cost-effectiveness into the design and construction process, DoD's greater emphasis on design-build construction and performance-based specifications present an opportunity for more-integrated design of high-performance facilities. The DOE and the National Renewable Energy Laboratory instituted a novel design-build performance contract for a LEED Platinum high-performance administrative building that delivered substantially reduced energy use but had costs that were comparable to other administrative buildings (DOE, 2012a; National Renewable Energy Laboratory, 2012; Pless and Torcellini, 2011). DoD may be able to achieve similar, competitive high-performance facilities through expanded emphasis on performance-based specifications. (See Table 2.8.)

Step 8: O&M and Decommissioning

Funding for facility maintenance and reinvestment is largely provided by the SRM accounts of the DoD budget. Facility operations funding is generally provided by Base Operations Support or other similar accounts in the DoD budget. Both DoD and installations have roles in O&M and decommissioning of facilities. DoD allocates O&M funding to installations based on square footage for each type of building. Installations receive the O&M funding and allocate it based on user needs. Several interviewees noted that SRM resources are typically provided as a reduced percentage

Table 2.8
Actors and Barriers to Life-Cycle Cost-Effective Facilities in the Design and Construction Stage

Actor	How Success Is Defined from Actor's Point of View	Barrier to Life-Cycle Cost-Effective Facilities
DoD construction agent field contract office	Facilities designed and constructed within schedule requirements and programmed amount of funding	Enforcement mechanisms for contractor failing to meet life-cycle cost obligations are unclear
DoD construction agent field engineering offices	Facilities designed and constructed to appropriate technical performance criteria	Resistant to design changes that increase initial costs
Contractors performing design and construction	Satisfied contract timing, performance, and cost requirements	Are not accountable for long-term cost performance of facilities
Installation user groups	Facilities designed and constructed meet user need and anticipated demands	Often value building enhancements and more space over reduced life-cycle costs

of their full calculated allocation, meaning that installations have to maintain facilities with fewer resources. Table 3 in the DoD Facilities Pricing Guide (UFC 3-701-01 as part of DoD, 2012a) lists estimates for several O&M cost categories by facility type. These include sustainment, water/wastewater, real property management, custodial services, refuse collection, grounds maintenance, pavement clearance, and pest control. Noticeably absent in Table 3 is an estimate of energy costs, which, while varying regionally, is nonetheless important for planning facilities. DoD advises that the costs in this table are for high-level planning and are not to be used during project estimating.

Installations have several disincentives toward pursuing life-cycle cost-effectiveness in operating and maintaining facilities. First, some O&M savings that they achieve, such as utilities expenses, would not necessarily accrue to the installation. This removes an immediate incentive that the installation might have for life-cycle cost-effectiveness and the savings it might bring. Second, decisions regarding facility repair, renovation, and new construction are informed through existing facility quality ratings. One interviewee told us that building-quality ratings can affect personnel ratings and suggested that this distorts the incentives of the personnel in charge of rating buildings toward favorable quality ratings. While we were unable to verify whether this personnel assertion is common practice in DoD for this study, it remains an important area for examination. If quality ratings were inflated, personnel could rate more favorably during a performance evaluation, while necessary facility O&M could be potentially deferred. DoD should examine the facility quality rating system to ensure that ratings are objective and verifiable, and that the incentives of actors involved are aligned with obtaining life-cycle cost-effective facilities. Independent audits of a limited sample of quality rating assessments could be a first step in this process.

It is also unclear how long life cycles of buildings may be and, therefore, what features of a facility may be life-cycle cost-effective. One interviewee told us, "People talk about life-cycle costs of 50 or 60 years. The services don't have an agreed-upon number for this, and it probably varies by facility type." (See Table 2.9.)

In this chapter, we described how the different entities, roles, and incentives associated with each step of a DoD facility's life cycle could potentially pose barriers to life-cycle cost-effectiveness. Meeting mission requirements at the best value to the government through the MILCON program involves maximizing the effectiveness of capital construction expenditures, often by finding ways to provide facilities for lower initial costs. Yet, decisions regarding facility elements and systems made during the planning, design, and construction phase ultimately affect funding requirements for operating and maintaining facilities over the facility's 25-year or greater operating life. DoD is currently incorporating many aspects of life-cycle cost-effectiveness throughout the process, especially when choosing building HVAC, plumbing, and other systems known to have high life-cycle costs. But barriers to achieving life-cycle cost-effective facilities are evident across the major steps in the process, stemming largely from the

Table 2.9
Actors and Barriers to Life-Cycle Cost-Effective Facilities in the O&M and Decommissioning Stage

Actor	How Success Is Defined from Actor's Point of View	Barrier to Life-Cycle Cost-Effective Facilities
Installation Department of Public Works	Facility is maintained at favorable quality rating with or below O&M funding allocated	May need to defer maintenance because of funding constraints
Installation or garrison commander	Needs of individuals served on the installation are met, and facilities receive favorable quality ratings	Personnel performance evaluation may be linked to facility quality ratings, which may not align with lowest life-cycle cost
Regional service organization	Mission requirements are met with high-quality facilities	Installation responsible for maintaining facilities
Service headquarters	O&M successfully maintains facilities with funding provided	O&M funding expense related to overall stock of facilities

fact that facility construction, operation, and maintenance funding is provided by different sources. Several interviewees noted that a pilot program to include total ownership costs is planned, which, depending on its complexity and costs to evaluate, could potentially assist in reducing life-cycle costs from DoD facilities.

Experimentation with new construction contracts, methods, and materials could, after lessons learned were incorporated, ultimately reveal processes to obtain facilities with lower life-cycle costs. Some choices, such as the type of structural materials used for facilities, are often dictated by building codes, as we discuss in the next chapter. But other choices, such as creative contracts and incentives, value-engineering exercises, high-performance standards, and data-informed total cost of ownership decisionmaking could potentially result in lower life-cycle costs. Interviewees expressed that there was substantial financial risk involved for installations and construction agents that attempted new facility designs and construction approaches. These risks include schedule delays, not meeting quality or cost expectations, and unexpected O&M costs for the facility's lifetime. There is tremendous institutional inertia, and there are incentives toward designing and constructing facilities that replicate previous projects that were viewed as a success. How success is defined depends on the actor involved, with completing a project on time and at or below the congressionally authorized facility cost being the primary objectives for many actors in the process.

CHAPTER THREE

The Role of Building Codes in Determining Construction Material

DoD, as noted earlier, constructs a wide variety of buildings. Between FY 2011 and FY 2013, DoD will construct nearly 1,000 new facilities and spend more than $25 billion to construct them (DoD, undated[a]). Table 3.1 lists the ten facility categories for which DoD appropriated the most construction funding between FY 2011 and FY 2013. Four facility categories of which DoD builds considerable numbers and to which it dedicates considerable construction appropriations are training buildings, enlisted unaccompanied personnel housing, airfield operational buildings, and aircraft maintenance facilities.

In this chapter, we examine the relationship between the facility category constructed and the type of building material chosen. We find that facility-specific building codes have a large role in dictating the building material used in construction. We also conclude that it is unclear how different types of building materials compare on life-cycle costs over the broad portfolio of DoD facilities, compared with similar institutional property owners.

The Role of the International Building Code and Building Types

In constructing buildings and choosing materials, DoD relies on the International Building Code (IBC). The IBC is a set of minimum safety standards for construction put forth and updated periodically by the International Code Council (International Code Council, 2012a). Many state and local governments use the IBC for their own regulations (International Code Council, 2012c). In 2002, DoD selected the IBC to guide MILCON.[1]

Much of the IBC deals with preventing fires and minimizing the impact of any that occur. Given these goals, the IBC limits the size of buildings, both in number of

---

[1] The guidance document that DoD then created for MILCON, UFC 1-200-01, Design: General Building Requirements, included both the current IBC rules and various other building standards on top of these (Facilities Management News, 2002).

Table 3.1
Top Ten DoD Facility Construction Categories by Appropriations, FY 2011 to FY 2013

Category	Number	Appropriation (in millions of dollars)[a]
Training buildings	161	2,845
Enlisted personnel unaccompanied housing	91	3,971
Airfield operational buildings	83	2,280
Aircraft maintenance facilities	75	2,360
Training ranges	70	473
Tank and automotive maintenance facilities	52	1,208
Administrative buildings	30	1,161
Ground operational buildings	23	511
Medical centers and hospitals	15	1,129
Communications buildings	15	475

[a] The ten categories shown in this table are ten of the top 11 categories as ranked by appropriation for construction between FY 2011 and FY 2013. Over this period, DoD is also building eight piers and wharfs with a total appropriation of $686 million, not included in Table 3.1.

SOURCE: FY 2013 Military Construction, Family Housing, and Base Realignment and Closure Program (C-1).

stories above ground and their square feet per story, based on their building type and usage. It specifies five construction types based on the combustibility of building materials and other elements. Table 3.2 summarizes these. Type I and Type II buildings must use noncombustible materials, such as concrete and steel, in their construction, with Type I buildings specifying a longer duration of fire resistance. Type III buildings must have noncombustible materials for exterior walls but may have other materials for other elements. Type IV buildings must also use noncombustible materials for their exterior walls but may use heavy timber, a type of wood construction with specific requirements in terms of materials and construction to confer fire resistance, for their other elements. Type V buildings may use combustible elements for both exterior and interior elements (International Code Council, 2012a).

There are ten broad categories of facility usage type—assembly, business, educational, factory, high-hazard, institutional, mercantile, storage, utility, and miscellaneous—with 26 subcategories. Usage type, building materials, and fire resistance of materials all help classify construction type. A facility proposed by private or public owners has a predetermined intended use, such as educational or institutional, and likely an intended size. If the proposed facility adheres to the IBC, the use category

Table 3.2
Construction Type and Materials

IBC Construction Type	Material Combustibility Requirements	Example Materials
Type I	Noncombustible for all building elements	Concrete, masonry, or steel
Type II	Noncombustible for all building elements	Concrete, masonry, or steel
Type III	Noncombustible for exterior walls; other elements may be combustible or noncombustible	Concrete, masonry, or steel for exterior; wood or other elements for interior
Type IV	Noncombustible for exterior walls; interior and certain exterior elements may be heavy timber	Masonry for exterior, heavy timber for interior
Type V	All elements may be combustible or noncombustible	Residential wood platform construction with exterior siding

SOURCES: International Code Council, 2012a; GAO, 2010.

and the size will dictate the construction type. For example, an elementary school or high school would be an educational facility. If an owner requires a three-story facility with at least 23,500 square feet per story, to adhere to the IBC, designers could propose a Type III facility, consisting of exterior load-bearing walls made with noncombustible materials with a layer of flame-retardant protection on specific building elements to increase their fire resistance rating (International Code Council, 2012a). The designer could also propose a Type I or II facility because of the increased level of fire protection but could not propose a Type IV or Type V facility without changing the use or reducing the size.

Table 3.3 shows how construction types can affect the maximum stories and square footage for four common types of DoD facilities: residential construction (such as for enlisted personnel unaccompanied housing), business (such as for an administration building), low-hazard storage (such as for a firehouse), and institutional (such as for a hospital). For any of these facilities, use of Type I materials would involve no restrictions on either stories or square footage. Beyond that, Type II generally allows larger facilities than Type III; Type III allows larger facilities, excepting business facilities, than Type IV; and Type IV allows larger facilities than Type V.

Adoption of the IBC means that MILCON is automatically restricted to certain building types and materials based on size and usage requirements. This means that many building material decisions are effectively made when building-size decisions are made, or before the RFP is issued.

For example, if a service decides to build one large residential building to house service members rather than a number of smaller residential buildings, it is constraining itself to certain building materials even if those evaluating the proposals have no

Table 3.3
Facility Use and Size Dictate Construction Type and Materials

	Residential (e.g., enlisted unaccompanied housing		Business (e.g., administration building)		Low-Hazard Storage (e.g., firehouse)		Institutional (e.g., hospital)	
	Maximum Permitted							
Type	Stories	Square Feet Per Story	Stories	Square Feet Per Story	Stories	Square Feet Per Story	Stories	Square Feet Per Story
I	Unlimited							
II	4	24,000	5	37,500	5	39,000	2	15,000
III	4	24,000	5	28,500	4	39,000	1	12,000
IV	4	20,500	5	36,000	5	38,500	1	12,000
V	3	12,000	3	18,000	4	21,000	1	9,500

SOURCES: International Code Council, 2012a; GAO, 2010; NAVFAC, 2008; U.S. Department of Veterans Affairs, 2007.

preference for such materials. A random Navy RFP that we reviewed for unaccompanied personnel housing, a commonly constructed type of building to house single service members, called for 250,000 square feet of space. Under the IBC, such a large residential building would require materials with fire-resistance ratings of two to three hours for both exterior and interior building elements (International Code Council, 2012a) or materials including masonry, concrete, and steel (Technical Services Information Bureau, 2008).

Table 3.4 illustrates the advantages and disadvantages that DoD may face in building two types of residential buildings. Should DoD build a Type I residential building, it can make it of any size it wishes but must use materials that are likely to be more expensive, increasing initial building costs (International Code Council, 2012b). Should DoD build a Type V residential building, it can use cheaper materials but must build a smaller facility.

Our interviewees had differing opinions on whether Type V construction could be substituted in circumstances in which DoD currently uses Type I construction. One

Table 3.4
Larger Residential Buildings Require More Capital-Intensive Materials

Type	Advantages	Disadvantages
I	Can be any size	Must use concrete, masonry, steel, and other more-expensive materials
V	Can use residential wood-platform construction with exterior siding	Cannot be larger than three stories and 12,000 square feet

interviewee said that there is a "tremendous amount of resistance" to using Type V construction for housing. "Everything has to be soldier-proofed. More of a commander's perception. There's a negative connotation with Type V design. Some of this is justified because of noise or vibration. But those could be mitigated with design. Go and look at hotels. They're all Type V." This view was verified in Marine Corps MILCON documents regarding unaccompanied personnel housing, which state, "Concrete Masonry Unit Block, while still not indestructible, is close, and therefore will be used in all bachelor enlisted quarters construction. There are no exceptions to this policy" (U.S. Marine Corps, 2010). Another interviewee concurred with the perception problem, saying that it "is one of the really big challenges to doing Type V construction. [Nobody] wants to be a guinea pig. I can't blame them. We've built a certain way for so long. So is it going to be durable?" Interviewees also expressed that they have had success with gaining acceptance of less commonly used military construction methods, such as Type V and prefabricated construction, after demonstrating these methods to local stakeholders for evaluation.

Another interviewee said that housing for soldiers should, in fact, be built with more durable materials, stating that military personnel require more resilient interior finishes: "It's more than just a family staying at a hotel with some suitcases." A fourth interviewee contended that evolving mission needs can require more durable construction materials, saying, "Typically for MILCON projects, which tend to be large buildings, we're going with two or three systems that we've found to be durable. And then, if there are mission changes in use—which there tend to be—we want building designs that don't require material changes. For instance, if we went with timber construction, but then the mission changes, we might not be able to use it."

Decisions to pursue buildings with more noncombustible materials might also be influenced by property insurance protocols and decisions. In general, federal facilities self-insure against potential property damages (GAO, 2004; Federal Register, 2011). Without property insurance, DoD facilities that suffer minor damage or a major loss would not have insurance funding available for reconstruction. The use of property insurance to mitigate risk in the private sector could be a contributing factor to different facility design and material choices than those used by DoD. The role of property insurance on risk and design choice is a worthwhile area for deeper examination.

In general, average construction costs per square foot are highest for construction Type I and progressively decrease for construction types II through V (International Code Council, 2012c). It is unclear how different types of building materials compare on life-cycle costs over the broad portfolio of DoD facilities. GAO (2010) examined construction materials usage by the services. The Army sought to reduce construction costs and time on some projects by switching construction materials from concrete, steel, and masonry to wood and by switching construction methods from on-site to modular construction. The Navy and Air Force continued to use concrete and steel materials and on-site construction, believing that these would reduce life-cycle costs.

The services did not, however, analyze which materials and methods would reduce overall life-cycle costs. The report found some preliminary evidence that wood-frame buildings might lead to construction and maintenance costs reductions, but it concluded that no long-term systematic evidence existed and recommended further study by the services (GAO, 2010).

In an earlier study, conducted in 2004, the National Association of Home Builders (NAHB) Research Center compared estimates of the life-cycle costs of barracks constructed with masonry and steel framing at Fort Detrick, Md., and barracks constructed with light wood-frame construction at Fort George G. Meade, Md. (NAHB Research Center, 2004). For each barracks, the authors estimated initial capital costs and salvage values, as well as maintenance, preventive maintenance, and capital improvements over a 40-year time frame. They found that, overall, the life-cycle cost estimates of the wood-frame barracks were about 40 percent lower than those of the masonry and steel barracks on a per square foot basis. The present value of initial construction costs was found to be about 37 percent lower in the wood-frame construction, while the present value of the maintenance, preventive maintenance, and capital improvements was about 55 percent lower in the wood-frame construction. However, the authors did not include utility costs in their estimation, which would be required to present a full life-cycle cost estimate between the two structures. Furthermore, considerable differences existed between the two facilities that may have affected the outcome. The Fort Meade wood-frame barracks were about three times the total square feet of the Fort Detrick barracks, which may have afforded some economies of scale in construction and maintenance on a per square foot basis. Additionally, the Fort Detrick masonry and steel barracks was constructed five years prior to the Fort Meade barracks, resulting in capital improvements required earlier in the facility's life-cycle.

As noted earlier, the Unified Facilities Criteria and Unified Facilities Guide Specifications ensure a prescribed level of performance and quality that contractors must provide. Contractors must meet these requirements regardless of the building type or material chosen by the contractor or dictated by the IBC. While DoD may be constrained by building type and size by the IBC, their control of the Unified Facilities Criteria and Unified Facilities Guide Specifications allows for continuous improvement in life-cycle cost optimization.

In our examination of DoD building material choices, we found that because DoD abides by the IBC, MILCON is automatically restricted to certain building types, and materials, based on size and usage requirements. As a result, many building material decisions are effectively made when building-size requirements decisions are made, or before the RFP is issued. It is also unclear how different types of building materials compare on life-cycle costs over the broad portfolio of DoD facilities, regions, and usage patterns. Interviewees expressed the need for objective data across services, rather than individual case studies, to determine the life-cycle cost-effectiveness of various building materials.

CHAPTER FOUR

Trade-Offs Between Annual O&M Costs and Initial Capital Costs

Analysts conducting life-cycle cost analyses estimate financial flows for a facility over its life and convert these flows into a present value.[1] This accounts for the time value of money, allowing decisionmakers to compare future financial obligations and current financial obligations among different projects. The value of future financial flows depends on the discount rate used in the analysis. For federal projects, the discount rate is set annually for various analysis periods by OMB (OMB, 2011), as well as by the National Institute of Standards and Technology and the DOE for energy and water conservation and renewable energy projects in federal facilities (Rushing et al., 2011). Accordingly, the *year* in which a life-cycle cost analysis is conducted affects the overall results and decisionmaking, as prescribed long-term discount rates fluctuate from year to year.

Some of our interviewees expressed a view that obtaining the lowest initial capital costs would generally yield the lowest life-cycle costs between alternatives, and, thus, DoD should focus on obtaining the lowest initial capital cost for projects. This hypothesis may hold true under certain conditions, such as large initial capital cost differences, small annual O&M flows, short analysis periods, or high discount rates. However, the DOE- and OMB-mandated discounted rates, which reflect the low cost of long-term U.S. government borrowing, coupled with facility lifetimes of 30 years or more, result in an increased importance of annual O&M financial flows for facilities in a life-cycle cost analysis. In Figure 4.1, we present an illustrative example of how discount rates and project lifetimes affect analysis outcomes. Using the real OMB discount rates for 20-year and 30-year projects,[2] and different facility lifetimes, we show on each line the expected annual O&M savings necessary to justify additional initial facility capital costs. Facilities with lower lifetimes (and hence lower OMB discount rates) will require

---

[1] Standard equations for converting future financial flows into present values can be found in most finance or construction management textbooks, as well as some government documents on life-cycle cost analysis—e.g., Hendrickson, 2008, and Rushing et al., 2011.

[2] The 2012 20-year and 30-year real rates are 1.7 percent and 2.0 percent, respectively. OMB guidance is to use the 30-year discount rate for any projects with a lifetime greater than 30 years (OMB, 2011).

Figure 4.1
Expected Annual O&M Savings Required to Justify Capital Cost Premiums

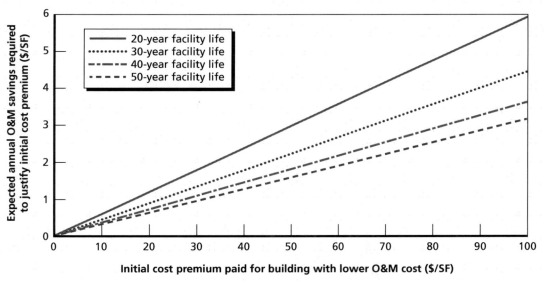

greater annual O&M savings to justify the same capital cost premiums as facilities with greater lifetimes, all else being equal. While this figure only includes initial capital costs and uniform annual O&M costs, it does illustrate that, in some cases, even large initial capital cost savings would not generate the lowest life-cycle costs if substantial annual O&M savings were expected. One interviewee told us that his or her perception was that the net present costs of an administrative building consisted of "about 65 percent initial costs, 20 percent sustainment, and 15 percent utilities." Ive (2006) estimates that the present value of office building O&M is about 1.5 times higher than initial construction costs, using a 7-percent discount rate.

The Army generally uses 25 years as the period of analysis in completing the economic analysis portion of DD Form 1391 (Smigel, 2010). While facility lifetime assumptions (and, hence, discount rates) will vary across individual facility types and projects, it is analytically imperative to use the same facility lifetime and discount rate assumptions within all aspects of each specific project analysis. When comparing two options within a specific project with different lifetimes (such as competing HVAC systems), engineering economic methods to annualize costs to compare options with unequal lifetimes can be used.

CHAPTER FIVE

Conclusions and Observations

Given the funds required to design, construct, operate, and maintain DoD facilities, Congress has issued statutory and regulatory guidance on obtaining life-cycle cost-effective facilities, and it recently expressed concerns that DoD construction methods and techniques may not obtain the most life-cycle cost-effective facilities. Our report provides a description of the process that DoD uses to obtain life-cycle cost-effective facilities and how that process affects DoD construction options and choices. The focus of our report is how the incentives and barriers of various actors involved affect the overall objective of obtaining life-cycle cost-effective facilities.

DoD is Currently Incorporating Life-Cycle Costing in Many Aspects of the MILCON Process

DoD, through its written design and acquisition policies and subsequent actions in the MILCON process, is currently incorporating many aspects of life-cycle cost-effectiveness. We found that DoD is conducting life-cycle cost analysis when choosing from the preliminary options of new construction, existing facility renovation, or facility leasing. The outcome of this analysis, which occurs early in the MILCON process, relies on the expertise of the personnel conducting the estimate and the quality of the assumptions and data used. Once an option is selected, we also found that there is clear guidance on selecting life-cycle cost-effective building systems, including energy, HVAC, and plumbing. Life-cycle cost decisionmaking procedures on these systems are provided by Unified Facility Criteria and Unified Facilities Guide Specifications documents, as well as DoD construction agent and other federal agency design guidelines and performance specifications, which guide contractors designing and constructing facilities. DoD also seeks to use Energy Star products or those certified by the DOE's Federal Energy Management Program in construction, which would reduce utility expenditures. In addition, applicable facilities are constructed to LEED Silver ratings, with DoD emphasizing to contractors the importance of the energy-savings aspects of these ratings. While these actions address a critical aspect of providing life-cycle cost-effective facilities, challenges and opportunities in the process remain.

Challenges in Obtaining Life-Cycle Cost-Effective Facilities

We found that several funding and organizational barriers across the institution create challenges in obtaining life-cycle cost-effective facilities. Over the life cycle of a facility, funding is required from three primary sources. New facility design and construction funding is overwhelmingly provided by congressional authorization and appropriation of MILCON projects. Funding for facility maintenance and reinvestment is largely provided by the SRM accounts of the DoD budget. Facility operations funding is generally provided by Base Operations Support or other similar accounts in the DoD budget. In addition, several entities are responsible for separate phases of a facility's life cycle, each with their own incentives and measures of success that together may not align with obtaining life-cycle cost-effective facilities. Meeting mission requirements at the best value to the government through the MILCON program involves maximizing the effectiveness of capital construction expenditures, often through finding ways to provide facilities for lower initial costs. However, decisions regarding facility elements and systems made during the planning, design, and construction phase ultimately affect funding requirements for operating and maintaining facilities over the facility's 25-year or greater operating life. For private-sector institutions that design, build, operate, and maintain their facilities, savings in any of these areas accrue to the organization, providing incentives for life-cycle cost decisionmaking. Since few or no opportunities to shift funding among the three primary DoD facility accounts exist, incentives toward lowering the overall costs to DoD are misaligned.

During our interviews and review of several MILCON RFP criteria, it is apparent that life-cycle cost criteria currently play little or no explicit role in the RFP evaluation criteria, with many RFPs including initial cost as a heavily weighted evaluation factor. Since contractors will deliver proposals and projects based on DoD evaluation criteria, adding life-cycle cost-effectiveness criteria to performance specifications and proposal-evaluation criteria could potentially obtain more life-cycle cost-effective facilities. However, interviewees told us that the challenges of incorporating nonstandard RFP evaluation criteria, such as those for life-cycle cost-effectiveness, may erode any potential benefits. In the limited time between RFP advertisement and due date (generally eight weeks), contractors would be required to develop justification for life-cycle cost elements of their proposed approach, either with their own internal proposal funding or through a qualified stipend from DoD. One interviewee said that in this time frame, "upfront decisions would be made that aren't necessarily cheap or fully researched, and we'll probably receive higher bids." Nonstandard evaluation factors require consensus on how to write the requirements and evaluation criteria for consistency and objectivity in judging proposals, further stressing time and resources. Interviewees were also very concerned with the prospect of verifying and enforcing contractor life-cycle cost savings claims made during the proposal, noting that if DoD identifies contractor-promised savings that fail to materialize several years after the facility is in operation, there are limited mechanisms to recover damages from contractors. Several interviewees noted that a DoD pilot program to include total ownership costs is planned, which, depending on its complexity and costs to evaluate, could potentially assist in reducing life-cycle costs from DoD facilities.

Despite the challenges of integrating life-cycle cost effectiveness into the design and construction process, DoD's greater emphasis on design-build construction and performance-based specifications presents an opportunity for more-integrated design of high-performance facilities. The DOE and the National Renewable Energy Laboratory experimented with a novel design-build performance contract for a LEED Platinum high-performance administrative building that delivered substantially reduced energy use but comparable costs to other administrative buildings (DOE, 2012a; National Renewable Energy Laboratory, 2012; Pless and Torcellini, 2011). DoD may be able to obtain similar, competitive high-performance facilities through expanded emphasis on performance-based specifications.

Several interviewees expressed that there was tremendous financial risk involved for installations and construction agents that attempt new facility designs and construction approaches. These risks include schedule delays, not meeting quality or cost expectations, and unexpected O&M costs for the life of the facility. There is tremendous institutional inertia, as well as incentives toward designing and constructing facilities that replicate previous projects that were viewed as a success. How success is defined depends on the actor involved, with completing a project on time and at or below the congressionally authorized facility cost being primary objectives for many actors in the process. Interviewees also expressed that they have had success with gaining acceptance of less commonly used military construction methods, such as wood-framed and prefabricated construction, after demonstrating these methods to local stakeholders for evaluation.

Observations and Potential Improvements

Obtaining life-cycle cost-effective facilities will ultimately produce cost savings for DoD, but these savings are achieved across three distinct funding sources: MILCON, SRM, and Base Operations Support. Finding methods to reward actors across these funding sources with a portion of life-cycle cost savings could incentivize greater focus on obtaining these facilities.

Just as sharing in potential benefits can incentivize life-cycle cost-effectiveness, actors can be incentivized by sharing in potential risks. Several interviewees expressed a desire for DoD construction agents and others making design and performance decisions to have a stake in the funding outcomes. Finding incentives to allow installations and designers to share in bid savings and greater use of performance-based contracting with a minimum square footage may be options for consideration. On a broad scale, this might involve congressional action to provide MILCON, SRM, and Base Operations Support funding in one single appropriation, with the ability to reprogram and optimize funding between these functions. On a more limited scale, Congress and DoD could analyze the life-cycle cost outcomes of the current very limited amounts of construction undertaken with SRM funding to examine whether outcomes differ from MILCON programing. Several interviewees suggested congressional authorization to conduct a greater amount of new facility construction with O&M funding, rather than MILCON funding.

As discussed, interviewees expressed that contractors would only focus on life-cycle costing if required, and adding these requirements would create challenges and the expenses of verifying and enforcing life-cycle cost-effectiveness claims proposed by contractors. However, a recent facility to house the U.S. Army Corps of Engineers (USACE) in Seattle, constructed for the General Services Administration, initiated a novel approach in performance contracting. The design-build construction contract includes a retainer of 0.5 percent of the contract value, in this case $330,000, which is only released to the contractor if energy use targets promised in the proposal are realized during a period after the facility becomes operational (Post, 2012). The results of this experiment can be evaluated after several years of building energy, usage, and other data are analyzed. DoD could obtain design, construction, and contracting lessons learned from this experiment and other performance-based contracting approaches undertaken by other government entities. These approaches, and other methods to incentivize building commissioning and verification of energy and other operating cost savings, may represent design and construction contracting tools available to DoD to realize at least a portion of promised life-cycle cost savings.

Aligning incentives during the O&M phase of the facility life cycle can also reduce costs. An interviewee noted the success of some services conducting walkthroughs on personnel housing at the end of a housing term and developing cost recovery methods from users for damages beyond normal usage. This is similar to procedures undertaken by many universities. If installations are accustomed to receiving reduced O&M funding allocations, incentives toward overdesigning facilities to reduce O&M expenditures will remain. In addition, decisions regarding facility repair, renovation, and new construction are informed through existing facility quality ratings. DoD should examine the facility quality rating system to ensure that ratings are objective and verifiable, and that the incentives of actors involved are aligned with obtaining life-cycle cost-effective facilities.

There was strong agreement among interviewees that Unified Facility Criteria, Unified Facilities Guide Specifications, and other service design guidelines drive the planning, design, and construction process for the MILCON program, and that enhancing these guidelines represents an opportunity to increase DoD's ability to obtain life-cycle cost-effective facilities. This allows value engineering and life-cycle cost estimations to be performed once and diffused into designs, rather than straining design resources by performing life-cycle cost estimations for each project. Furthermore, interviewees stated that DoD-wide life-cycle cost estimations that are affected by regional differences could be performed on a regional basis.

In addition to improving standards and performance guidelines, several interviewees felt that large improvements could be made in the planning and design phases, with one interviewee adding that life-cycle cost analysis for MILCON projects "is best applied in the planning and design phase as part of developing a refined standard design using a structured value engineering/value management process." As discussed, very limited technical details regarding proposed projects are available to planners and designers until after projects are authorized and appropriated by Congress. Hence, opportunities to institutionalize life-cycle cost analysis across the services are likely to have a greater impact than simply requiring each project to undertake a resource-intensive initiative. This could involve data-based life cycle cost inputs to the Unified Facilities Criteria and Unified Facilities Guide Specifications documents, incorporating total cost of ownership data into the project development and decisionmaking process, and design specialization. Several interviewees noted that opportunities for design specialization and standardization across services exist. This could include establishing a single design center for each major facility type in one DoD construction agency that serves all the services. These design centers would, as one interviewee suggested, "be responsible and held accountable for tracking the holistic performance of all their facilities to optimize mission accomplishment and life-cycle costs. Only a dedicated design center would have the resources to effectively collect and implement lessons learned, stay current with industry trends, and to develop and revise . . . a standard design." Private-sector owners of large numbers of similar facilities use design standardization, which enables continuous design improvement and greater life-cycle cost performance tracking and comparison across their portfolio. In addition, life-cycle cost-effectiveness decisions are greatly affected by assumptions, methods, and regional variables, all of which a single design center could standardize and document. One group of interviewees disagreed that design standardization could broadly enhance life-cycle cost-effectiveness, as it would discourage risk. Therefore, it is important that any design standardization be adaptable to new technologies and provides opportunities for locally led efficiencies.

We also examined the process issues related to use of different building materials in construction. In constructing buildings and choosing materials, DoD relies on the IBC, a set of minimum safety standards for construction put forth and updated periodically by the International Code Council. Much of the IBC deals with preventing fires and minimizing the impact of any that occur. Given these goals, the IBC limits the size of buildings, both in number of stories above ground and their square feet per story, based on the building type and usage. It specifies five construction types based on the combustibility of building materials and other elements. Adoption of the IBC means that MILCON is automatically restricted to certain building types and materials, based on size and usage requirements. This means that many building material decisions are effectively made when building-size requirements decisions are made, or before the RFP is issued. An exception is the Marine Corps, which has a relatively small proportion of DoD facilities. The Marine Corps has a policy requiring concrete masonry unit block for interior walls of enlisted quarters (U.S. Marine Corps, 2010). The Marine Corps utilizes concrete or block interior walls to reduce what it perceives to be the high maintenance costs of other materials. We note that the appropriate level of fire protection for DoD facilities is an important area for future research, but deviating from the current level of fire protection to reduce life-cycle costs would only be prudent if overall casualty risk from fires did not increase.

In general, average construction costs per square foot are lower for facilities constructed with combustible materials than for facilities with higher levels of fire protection. It is unclear how different types of building materials compare on life-cycle costs over the broad portfolio of DoD facilities, regions, and usage patterns. The GAO (2010) examined construction materials usage by the services. It found some preliminary evidence that wood-frame buildings might lead to reduced construction and maintenance costs but concluded that no long-term systematic evidence existed and recommended further study by the services. Our interviewees echoed this view, noting wide variation in materials, usage, and outcomes. Interviewees expressed the need for objective data across services, rather than individual case studies, to determine the life-cycle cost-effectiveness of various building materials.

In this analysis, we have characterized the process that DoD uses to obtain life-cycle cost-effective facilities and identified misaligned incentives and barriers in this process. Yet, a full analysis measuring the extent to which DoD is obtaining life-cycle cost-effective facilities would require facility-level capital and O&M expenditures data over a time frame sufficient to understand and project cost trends. Using these data and analytically controlling for exogenous factors—such as how regional weather affects heating and cooling needs—an estimation of the impacts of different building designs, materials, and systems on life-cycle costs could be obtained. Annually updated facility-level life-cycle costs could also enable performance comparisons across facility, region, and construction agency. Many universities approach facility asset management by cataloging each maintenance service call for each facility, measuring facility-specific utility consumption and other data-gathering processes to inform detailed life-cycle cost decisionmaking. Having credible and verifiable cost data to establish DoD baselines for comparison was identified by a recent National Research Council report (NRC, 2013) evaluating the cost-effectiveness of sustainable building standards used by DoD. However, the DoD-wide collection and analysis of these detailed data in the near term would be resource- and time-intensive for DoD. The potential magnitude and budgetary impact of the additional life-cycle cost savings are also unclear, given that constructing, operating, and maintaining facilities generally has represented about 2–4 percent of the DoD budget. Given this reality, in addition to the performance-based specifications and enhancements to life-cycle cost standard and guidelines discussed, an effort to benchmark DoD facility costs using existing available data could assist current decisionmaking, and DoD could incorporate new data as they become available. Benchmarking would include characterizing capital and O&M expenditures by facility type for a limited set of facilities, both within and across services, as well as against comparable institutional facility owners. With additional data, DoD could expand its use of asset management metrics for facilities (similar to those proposed in IFMA, 2008) to compare facility costs and performance across and within the services and DoD construction agencies. This effort could potentially identify performance trends, maintenance expense "hot spots," and best practices for design and construction. Benchmarking facilities against those constructed by institutional and private-sector peers could help establish performance metrics to encourage innovation in DoD's effort to obtain life-cycle cost-effective facilities.

RAND Interview Protocol Used in this Research

Assessing Effective Life-Cycle Costs for Military Construction: Guide for Interviews

In the National Defense Authorization Act for FY 2011, Congress asked the Office of the Deputy Under Secretary of Defense for Installations and Environment (ODUSD[I&E]) to assess effective life-cycle costs for military construction. In support of DoD's response to Congress, RAND was asked by ODUSD(I&E) to provide an independent analysis to characterize DoD's *process* of obtaining life-cycle cost-effective buildings.

Below, we provide background on our project and a list of questions as a guide to the type of information we hope to obtain during our interviews. The questions below are intended for use by the two RAND researchers leading this project, to help guide a conversation with interviewees. The open-ended discussion can focus on topics where the interviewees have expertise and interest. The conversation is particularly beneficial to our research, and hence we are not asking for a written response to these questions. In reporting the results of this study, individuals who are interviewed will not be associated with their specific responses.

Project Background

Title 10, United States Code, requires the military construction planning and acquisition process to incorporate life-cycle cost-effective practices to minimize total project costs over the life of the facility. Section 2801 of Title 10, United States Code, considers a facility life-cycle cost-effective if the estimated total present value of a facility's investment costs, capital costs, installation costs, energy costs, operating costs, maintenance costs, and replacement costs does not exceed an established baseline comparison. House Report 111-491, accompanying the National Defense Authorization Act for FY 2011 (page 505), expressed concerns that the varying construction methods and materials used by DoD may not obtain the most life-cycle cost-effective facilities. These include the use of wood-framed materials rather than traditional concrete, steel, and masonry construction, as well as the use of modular construction techniques. Among the many factors that can influence life-cycle costs are facility and system design, construction methods, contracting methods employed, estimates used to generate life-cycle cost analyses, and maintenance patterns. Congress requested DoD to provide

1. an evaluation of the current construction techniques used by DoD to achieve life-cycle cost-effective facilities
2. a comparison of DoD and industry construction methods
3. an assessment of the effectiveness of contract provisions to obtain life-cycle cost-effective facilities
4. an assessment of the effectiveness of DoD to obtain the life-cycle cost-effective assessment established pursuant to Section 2801 of Title 10, United States Code
5. a recommendation of the most effective life-cycle period, by facility type, that DoD should use to obtain the most cost-effective facilities.

Interviews with various stakeholders are essential to supporting DoD's response to Congress, and below are the types of issues we would like to discuss. We recognize that not all stakeholders will have experience with all of these issues, and we will focus on specific areas of expertise with each interviewee.

Questions Regarding Proposal Development

Please tell us about the proposal development process:

- Do the facility design and construction requests for proposals (RFPs) originate in your office?
- Does your office amend or edit the RFP?
- Who defines the specifications for the RFP, and what criteria are used in specification creation?
- Are life-cycle costs defined in the RFP? If so, how are they defined?
- Are life-cycle costs requested and considered in the RFP? Is the importance of life-cycle costs defined and weighted in the RFP?
- Are construction types (Types I–V) included or excluded in the specifications?
- Are prefabricated construction methods included or excluded in the specifications?

Questions Regarding Economic Analyses and DD Form 1391

Please tell us about the economic analyses process:

- Does your office prepare or evaluate DD Form 1391 for facility capital construction projects?
- Does your office complete or evaluate economic analyses or other life-cycle cost analyses for facility capital construction projects?
- Is a software package used for the economic analyses or other life-cycle cost analyses? Which one?

- What is the design service life (years) that is assumed on economic analyses or other life-cycle cost analyses? Is sensitivity analysis conducted?

Questions Regarding Proposal Evaluation

Please tell us about the proposal evaluation process:

- Does your office evaluate facility design and construction proposals?
- What are the primary staff titles evaluating proposals? Do they have engineering or construction training?
- Are life-cycle costs an official criterion for evaluation? What is their weighting in evaluation?
- Are building construction type or materials an official criterion for evaluation? What is their weighting in evaluation?
- How would a decision be made between two proposals of similar quality but trade-offs in capital costs versus life-cycle costs?
- Have Type III, IV, or V construction using wood framed structures been proposed on projects within the last three years? Have any been awarded? Why or why not?
- Have prefabricated construction methods been proposed on projects within the last three years? Have any been awarded? Why or why not?

Questions Regarding Construction Methods and Materials

Please tell us about the process of specifying construction methods and materials:

- How do engineers and contractors propose and deliver life-cycle cost-effective structures?
- Have Type III, IV, or V construction using wood framed structures been used on projects within the last three years? Have any been awarded? Why or why not?
- Have prefabricated construction methods been used on projects within the last three years? Have any been awarded? Why or why not?
- Do construction methods and materials vary across regions?

Questions Regarding O&M

- What are the major O&M costs for facilities? Do they vary by construction type or material?
- Do reports about high O&M costs at existing facilities from facility managers influence language in newly issued RFPs?

Navy MILCON Team Planning and Programming Process Diagram

Figure B.1
Navy MILCON Team Planning and Programming Process Diagram

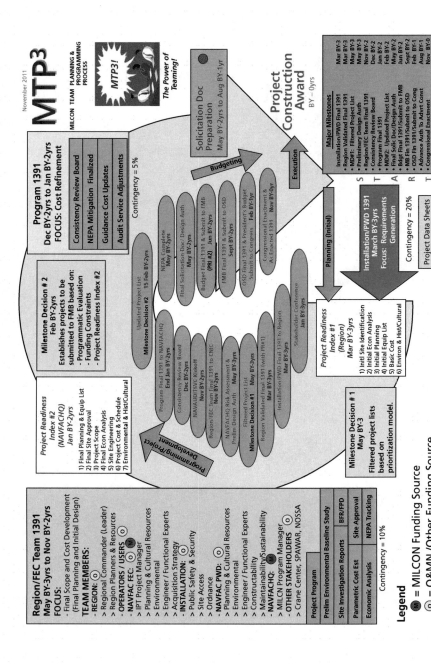

SOURCE: Provided by interviewees in December 2011. A 2008 version of this chart is available in Nesius (2011).

RAND RR169-B.1

Sample U.S. Army DD Form 1391

Figure C.1
Sample U.S. Army DD Form 1391, Page 1 of 3

1. COMPONENT	FY 2013 MILITARY CONSTRUCTION PROJECT DATA		2. DATE
ARMY			01 AUG 2011 21 JAN 2010

3. INSTALLATION AND LOCATION	4. PROJECT TITLE
Fort Huntsville Alabama	Maintenance Shop, General Purpose

5. PROGRAM ELEMENT	6. CATEGORY CODE	7. PROJECT NUMBER	8. PROJECT COST ($000)
	218 85	80321	49,000

9. COST ESTIMATES

ITEM	U/M	QUANTITY	UNIT COST	COST ($000)
PRIMARY FACILITY				37,388
Administration and Shop Control, DOL/DPW/I	SF	8,000	145.53	(1,164)
Maintenance Shop, General Purpose	SF	60,000	136.82	(8,209)
Vehicle Maintenance Shop - Wheeled	SF	35,000	192.08	(6,723)
Vehicle Maintenance Shop - Track	SF	25,000	199.38	(4,985)
Engineering/Housing Maintenance Shop	SF	35,000	143.21	(5,012)
Total from Continuation page(s)				(11,295)
SUPPORTING FACILITIES				5,419
Electric Service	LS	--	--	(1,080)
Water, Sewer, Gas	LS	--	--	(819)
Paving, Walks, Curbs And Gutters	LS	--	--	(3,080)
Storm Drainage	LS	--	--	(19)
Site Imp(133) Demo(154)	LS	--	--	(287)
Information Systems	LS	--	--	(89)
Antiterrorism Measures	LS	--	--	(46)
ESTIMATED CONTRACT COST				42,807
CONTINGENCY (5.00%)				2,140
SUBTOTAL				44,947
SUPERVISION, INSPECTION & OVERHEAD (5.70%)				2,562
DESIGN/BUILD - DESIGN COST (4.0000%)				1,798
TOTAL REQUEST				49,307
TOTAL REQUEST (ROUNDED)				49,000
INSTALLED EQT-OTHER APPROPRIATIONS				(2,476)

10. Description of Proposed Construction
   Construct a Maintenance Facility complex. Project includes wheeled and
track vehicle maintenance facilities, housing maintenance facility,
electronic, battery, and machine shops, organizational vehicle parking,
organizational storage, petroleum and other hazardous materiel storage,
information systems, fire protection and alarm systems, Intrusion Detection
System (IDS)installation, and Energy Monitoring Control Systems (EMCS)
connection. Supporting facilities include site development, utilities and
connections, lighting, paving, parking, walks, curbs and gutters, storm
drainage, information systems, landscaping and signage. Heating and air
conditioning will be provided by connection to the existing energy plant.
Measures in accordance with the Department of Defense (DoD) Minimum
Antiterrorism for Buildings standards will be provided. Demolish 2 buildings
(48,000 Total SF). Air Conditioning (Estimated 48 Tons).

DD FORM 1391 1 DEC 76	PREVIOUS EDITIONS MAY BE USED INTERNALLY UNTIL EXHAUSTED	PAGE NO. 1

SOURCE: USACE, 2012.
RAND *RR169-c.1*

Figure C.2
Sample U.S. Army DD Form 1391, Page 2 of 3

1. COMPONENT ARMY	FY 2013 MILITARY CONSTRUCTION PROJECT DATA	2. DATE 01 AUG 2011 21 JAN 2010

3. INSTALLATION AND LOCATION
Fort Huntsville
Alabama

4. PROJECT TITLE	5. PROJECT NUMBER
Maintenance Shop, General Purpose	80321

9.   COST ESTIMATES (CONTINUED)

Item	U/M	Qty	Unit Cost	Cost ($000)
PRIMARY FACILITY (CONTINUED)				11,295
Electronics Maintenance Shop	SF	10,000	147.51	(1,475)
Battery Shop	SF	5,000	130.73	(654)
Machine Shop	SF	10,000	185.22	(1,852)
Quality Assurance/Calibration Facility, Ge	SF	5,000	131.28	(656)
Hazardous Material Storage	SF	2,000	177.57	(355)
Storage Facility, General Purpose	SF	15,000	119.07	(1,786)
Organizational Vehicle Parking, Surfaced	SY	32,000	75.31	(2,410)
Sustainability/Energy Measures	LS	--	--	(718)
Antiterrorism Measures	LS	--	--	(718)
Building Information Systems	LS	--	--	(671)

11. REQ: 210,000 SF ADQT: 140,000 SF SUBSTD: 70,000 SF
PROJECT:
    Construct a Maintenance Facility complex.

REQUIREMENT:
    Currently, maintenance is handled at 15 separate facilities which do not
meet safety standards. A consolidated facility will offer safe working
conditions, provide centralized customer service, and eliminate redundant
services.

CURRENT SITUATION:
    There are 15 existing facilities with 210,000 SF of space scattered across
a 5-mile radius.

IMPACT IF NOT PROVIDED:
    Maintenance will continue to be performed in scattered, substandard
facilities. Soldiers will continue performing maintenance in hazardous
conditions. Customers will continue needing to go to one of 15 different
locations, depending on their specific maintenance need.

ADDITIONAL:
    This project has been coordinated with the installation physical security
plan, and all physical security measures are included. All required
antiterrorism protection measures are included. Alternative methods of meeting
this requirement have been explored during project development. This project
is the only feasible option to meet the requirement. The Deputy Assistant
Secretary of the Army (Installations, Housing and Partnerships) certifies that

DD FORM 1391C 1 DEC 76   PREVIOUS EDITIONS MAY BE USED INTERNALLY UNTIL EXHAUSTED   PAGE NO.   2

Figure C.3
Sample U.S. Army DD Form 1391, Page 3 of 3

1. COMPONENT	FY 2013 MILITARY CONSTRUCTION PROJECT DATA	2. DATE
ARMY		01 AUG 2011
		21 JAN 2010

3. INSTALLATION AND LOCATION
Fort Huntsville
Alabama

4. PROJECT TITLE	5. PROJECT NUMBER
Maintenance Shop, General Purpose	80321

```
ADDITIONAL:    (CONTINUED)
this project has been considered for joint use potential. The facility will be
available for use by other components.




                                            PAX Team



ESTIMATED CONSTRUCTION START:          MAR 2013              INDEX: 2622
ESTIMATED MIDPOINT OF CONSTRUCTION:    SEP 2013              INDEX: 2644
ESTIMATED CONSTRUCTION COMPLETION:     MAR 2014              INDEX: 2668
```

DD FORM 1391C 1 DEC 76	PREVIOUS EDITIONS MAY BE USED INTERNALLY UNTIL EXHAUSTED	PAGE NO. 3

SOURCE: USACE, 2012.

RAND RR169-c.3

Bibliography

Adams, Regina Renee, *Resourcing the Force: What Is Funded Versus Actually Received*, U.S. Army War College, 2008.

American Society of Heating, Refrigeration and Air-Conditioning Engineers (ASHRE), "Advanced Energy Design Guide for Small to Medium Office Buildings," 2011.

California Legislative Analyst's Office, "Design-Build: An Alternative Construction System," State of California, February 3, 2005. As of May 25, 2012:
http://www.lao.ca.gov/2005/design_build/design_build_020305.htm

CDM Smith, "Supporting Military Preparedness," 2012. As of October 8, 2012:
http://cdmsmith.com/en-US/Solutions/Water/Supporting%20Military%20Preparedness.aspx

Christensen, Paul N., Gordon A. Sparks, and Kent J. Kostuk, "A Method-Based Survey of Life Cycle Costing Literature Pertinent to Infrastructure Design and Renewal," *Canadian Journal of Civil Engineering*, Vol. 32, No. 1, 2005, pp. 250–259.

Defense Acquisition University (DAU), "Planning, Programming, Budgeting, & Execution: Budgeting Phase," undated. As of May 14, 2012:
https://learn.dau.mil/CourseWare/10_7/mod4/au4/m0404_b0030.html

DiStasio, Jr., Frank A., *Army Budget: An Analysis, Fiscal Year 2012*, The Association of the United States Army, Arlington, Va., 2011. As of May 7, 2012:
http://www.ausa.org/publications/ilw/Documents/Budget_Book_FY12_web.pdf

DoD—*see* U.S. Department of Defense.

DOE—*see* U.S. Department of Energy.

Eichholtz, Piet, Nils Kok, and John M. Quigley, "Doing Well by Doing Good? Green Office Buildings," *American Economic Review*, Vol. 100, No. 5, 2010, pp. 2492–2509.

———, "The Economics of Green Building," *Review of Economics and Statistics*, 2012.

Facilities Management News, "Defense Department Chooses International Building Code to Standardize Military Construction," August 26, 2002. As of May 8, 2012:
http://www.fmlink.com/News/ArchivedArticles/DefenseD.13687.html

Federal Register, Defense Federal Acquisition Regulation Supplement: Responsibility and Liability for Government Property (DFARS Case 2010-D018), 76 FR 71823-71826. November 18, 2011. As of November 28, 2012:
https://federalregister.gov/a/2011-29416

Fuller, Sieglinde, "Guidance on Life-Cycle Cost Analysis Required by Executive Order 13123," National Institute of Standards and Technology, for U.S. Department of Energy, April 2005. As of May 7, 2012:
http://www1.eere.energy.gov/femp/pdfs/lcc_guide_05.pdf

———, "Life-Cycle Cost Analysis (LCCA)," National Institute of Standards and Technology, Hosted by the Whole Building Design Guide, June 28, 2010. As of May 7, 2012:
http://www.wbdg.org/resources/lcca.php

Fuller, Sieglinde, and Steven R. Petersen, "Life Cycle Costing Manual for the Federal Energy Management Program," National Institute of Standards and Technology, NIST Handbook 135, 1995. As of May 7, 2012:
www.nist.gov/customcf/get_pdf.cfm?pub_id=907459

FY 2013 Military Construction, Family Housing, and Base Realignment and Closure Program (C-1), undated. As of January 30, 2013:
http://comptroller.defense.gov/defbudget/fy2013/c1.xlsx

GAO—see Government Accountability Office.

Gluch, Pernilla, and Henrikke Baumann, "The Life Cycle Costing (LCC) Approach: A Conceptual Discussion of Its Usefulness for Environmental Decision-Making," *Building and Environment,* Vol. 39, No. 5, 2004, pp. 571–580.

Government Accountability Office, "States Are Experimenting with Design-Build Contracting," April 29, 1997. As of May 7, 2012:
http://www.gao.gov/products/RCED-97-138R

———, "Principles of Federal Appropriations Law: Third Edition, Volume I," January 2004. As of November 28, 2012:
http://www.gao.gov/products/GAO-04-261SP

———, "Defense Infrastructure: Continued Management Attention Is Needed to Support Installation Facilities and Operations," April 24, 2008. As of October 8, 2012:
http://www.gao.gov/products/GAO-08-502

———, "Defense Infrastructure: DoD Needs to Determine and Use the Most Economical Building Materials and Methods When Acquiring New Permanent Facilities," April 2010. As of May 7, 2012:
http://www.gao.gov/new.items/d10436.pdf

Helgeson, Jennifer F., and Barbara C. Lippiatt, "Multidisciplinary Life Cycle Metrics and Tools for Green Buildings," *Integrated Environmental Assessment and Management*, Vol. 5, No. 3, 2009, pp. 390–398.

Hendrickson, Chris T., "Project Management for Construction: Fundamental Concepts for Owners, Engineers, Architects and Builders," Version 2.2, e-book, 2008. First printing by Prentice Hall with co-author Tung Au, 1989. As of May 8, 2012:
http://pmbook.ce.cmu.edu/

House Report 111-491—see U.S. House of Representatives.

International Code Council, *International Building Code*, 2012a. As of May 8, 2012:
http://publicecodes.citation.com/icod/ibc/index.htm

———, "Building Valuation Data," February 2012b. As of May 8, 2012:
http://www.iccsafe.org/cs/Pages/BVD.aspx

———, "Adoption by State," July 2012c. As of May 8, 2012:
http://www.iccsafe.org/gr/documents/stateadoptions.pdf

International Facility Management Association (IFMA), "Asset Lifecycle Model for Total Cost of Ownership Management: Framework, Glossary, and Definitions," 2008. As of February 20, 2013: http://www.ifma.org/docs/knowledge-base/asset_lifecyle_model.pdf?sfvrsn=2

Ive, Graham, "Re-Examining the Costs and Value Ratios of Owning and Occupying Buildings," *Building Research & Information,* Vol. 34, No. 3, 2006, pp. 230–245.

Keoleian, Gregory A., Steven Blanchard, and Peter Reppe, "Life-Cycle Energy, Costs, and Strategies for Improving a Single-Family House," *Journal of Industrial Ecology,* Vol. 4, No. 2, 2000, pp. 135–156.

Kibert, Charles J., *Sustainable Construction: Green Building Design and Delivery,* John Wiley and Sons, 2008.

Kneifel, Joshua, "Life-Cycle Carbon and Cost Analysis of Energy Efficiency Measures in New Commercial Buildings," *Energy and Buildings,* Vol. 42, No. 3, 2010, pp. 333–340.

———, "Beyond the Code: Energy, Carbon, and Cost Savings Using Conventional Technologies," *Energy and Buildings,* Vol. 43, No. 4, 2011, pp. 951–959.

Korpi, Eric, and Timo Ala-Risku, "Life Cycle Costing: A Review of Published Case Studies," *Managerial Auditing Journal,* Vol. 23, No. 3, 2008, pp. 240–261.

McMillan, Lauren Ashley, "Analysis of Naval Facilities Engineering Command Military Construction Projects and the Overall Military Construction Process," M.S. thesis, University of Texas at Austin. August 2005. As of December 3, 2011: http://www.dtic.mil/cgi-bin/GetTRDoc?AD=ADA447058

Montanya, Eduard Cubi, and David W. Keith, "LEED, Energy Savings, and Carbon Abatement: Related but Not Synonymous," *Environmental Science & Technology,* Vol. 45, No. 5, 2011, pp. 1757–1758.

NAHB Research Center—*see* National Association of Home Builders Research Center.

National Association of Home Builders Research Center, "Comparison of Life Cycle Costs of UEPH at Fort George G. Meade and Fort Detrick," August 12, 2004.

National Renewable Energy Laboratory, "Research Support Facility," June 11, 2012. As of June 11, 2012: http://www.nrel.gov/sustainable_nrel/rsf.html

National Research Council (NRC), *Investments in Federal Facilities: Asset Management Strategies for the 21st Century,* Washington, D.C.: The National Academies Press, 2004.

———, *Achieving High-Performance Federal Facilities: Strategies and Approaches for Transformational Change,* Washington, D.C.: The National Academies Press, 2011.

———, *Energy-Efficiency Standards and Green Building Certification Systems Used by the Department of Defense for Military Construction and Major Renovations,* Washington, D.C.: The National Academies Press, 2013. As of February 20, 2013: http://www.nap.edu/catalog.php?record_id=18282

Naval Facilities Command (NAVFAC), "NAVFAC SE Interim Design Guidance: Integrating Energy and Water Efficiencies into Contracts," February 1, 2012. As of May 25, 2012: https://portal.navfac.navy.mil/portal/page/portal/navfac/navfac_ww_pp/navfac_southeast_pp/about_us/tech_specs/navfac%20se%20interim%20design%20guidance%202-1-12.pdf

———, "National Naval Medical Center, Master Plan Update 2008," November 7, 2008. As of February 20, 2013: http://www6.montgomerycountymd.gov/content/exec/brac/pdf/master_plan-fileone-082608.pdf

Naval Facilities Engineering Command, "LEED for New Construction v3.0 Workbook," undated. As of January 13, 2013:
http://www.wbdg.org/docs/relational_tool.xls

NAVFAC—*see* Naval Facilities Command.

Neuhaus, Bryan K., Kristie L. Bissell, Brian H. Greenhalgh, James L. Hathaway, and Amita Singh, "Unaccompanied Personnel Housing for Junior Enlisted Members," Report HCS80T1, LMI, MacLean, Va., 2010. As of October 8, 2012:
www.acq.osd.mil/housing/UPH%20Report.pdf

Nesius, John J., "NAVFAC Washington Overview: MILCON and BRAC Program Status," presented to the Design-Build Institute of America Mid-Atlantic Region, May 17, 2011. As of May 25, 2012:
http://www.dbia-mar.org/downloads/DBIA%20Brief%2017%20MAY%202011.pdf

Newsham, Guy R., Sandra Mancini, and Benjamin J. Birt, "Do LEED-Certified Buildings Save Energy? Yes, But . . . ," *Energy and Buildings*, Vol. 41, No. 8, August 2009, pp. 897–905.

NRC—*see* National Research Council.

Office of Management and Budget, Capital Programming Guide, version 2.0, supplement to OMB Circular A-11, Part 7 on Planning, Budgeting, and Acquisition of Capital Assets, June 2006.

———, Circular A-11, Part 7, Planning, Budgeting, Acquisition, and Management of Capital Assets, June 2008.

———, Circular A-94, Appendix C, Discount Rates for Cost-Effectiveness, Lease Purchase, and Related Analyses, revised December 2011. As of May 2, 2012:
http://www.whitehouse.gov/omb/circulars_a094/a94_appx-c

OMB—*see* Office of Management and Budget.

Pearce, Annie R., "Sustainable Capital Projects: Leapfrogging the First Cost Barrier," *Civil Engineering and Environmental Systems,* Vol. 25, No. 4, 2008, pp. 291–300.

Pearce, Annie R., Kristen L. S. Bernhardt, and Michael J. Garvin, "Sustainability and Socio-Enviro-Technical Systems: Modeling Total Cost of Ownership in Capital Facilities," *Proceedings of the IEEE 2010 Winter Simulation Conference*, 2010, pp. 3157–3169.

Pless, Shanti, and Paul Torcellini, "Controlling Capital Costs in High-Performance Office Buildings," U.S. Department of Energy, October 31, 2011. As of June 1, 2012:
http://www1.eere.energy.gov/buildings/alliances/webinar_capitalcost_20111031_text.html

Post, Nadine, M., "Fee Holdback Raises Eyebrows," *Engineering News Record*, May 14, 2012.

Rushing, Amy, S., Joshua D. Kneifel, and Barbara C. Lippiatt, "Energy Price Indices and Discount Factors for Life-Cycle Cost Analysis—2011, Annual Supplement to NIST Handbook 135 and NBS Special Publication 709," National Institute of Standards and Technology, NISTIR 85-3273-76-26, hosted by the Whole Building Design Guide, September 2011. As of February 9, 2012:
http://wbdg.org/ccb/DOE/TECH/nistir85_3273_26.pdf

Scofield, John H., "Do LEED-Certified Buildings Save Energy? Not Really . . . ," *Energy and Buildings*, Vol. 41, No. 12, December 2009, pp. 1386–1390.

Smigel, Donna R., "Manual for Preparation of Economic Analyses for Military Construction (and Base Realignment and Closure [BRAC])," U.S. Army Corps of Engineers, April 2010. As of December 3, 2011:
http://140.194.146.135/CEMP/Econ/Documents/WEB_EAManualApril2010.pdf

Stuban, Steven M.F, Thomas A. Mazzuchi, and Shahram Sarkani, "Employing Risk Management to Control Military Construction Costs," Defense Acquisition University, April 2011. As of June 12, 2012:
http://www.dtic.mil/dtic/tr/fulltext/u2/a539719.pdf

Stumpf, Annette L., Julie L. Webster, Richard L. Schneider, Elisabeth M. Jenicek, Justine A. Kane, and Kelly L. Fishman, "Integration of Sustainable Practices into Standard Army MILCON Designs," U.S. Army Corps of Engineers, ERDC/CERL TR-11-27, September 2011. As of May 14, 2011:
http://www.dtic.mil/dtic/tr/fulltext/u2/a550493.pdf

Technical Services Information Bureau, "IBC Building Types," September 2008. As of May 8, 2012:
http://www.tsib.org/pdf/technical/10-101_Building_Codes.pdf

United States Code, Title 10, Section 2801.

U.S. Air Force, "The United States Air Force Project Manager's Guide for Design and Construction," June 1, 2000. As of December 2, 2011:
http://www.sheppard.af.mil/shared/media/document/AFD-061229-027.pdf

———, "Planning and Programming Military Construction (MILCON) Projects," June 14, 2010. As of December 2, 2011:
http://www.wbdg.org/ccb/AF/AFI/afi_32_1021.pdf

———, "Financial Management Economic Analysis," Air Force Manual 65-506, August 29, 2011. As of May 2, 2011:
http://www.af.mil/shared/media/epubs/AFMAN65-506.pdf

U.S. Army, "Army Facilities Management," Army Regulation 420-1, March 28, 2009a. As of December 2, 2011:
http://www.apd.army.mil/pdffiles/r420_1.pdf

———, "Army Military Construction and Nonappropriated-Funded Construction Program Development and Execution," Army Regulation 420-1-2, April 2, 2009b. As of December 2, 2011:
http://www.apd.army.mil/pdffiles/p420_1_2.pdf

U.S. Army Corps of Engineers, "Design Build Instructions (DBI) for Military Construction," CEMP-EA, October 29, 1994. As of May 8, 2012:
http://www.wbdg.org/ccb/ARMYCOE/DBI/ARCHIVES/cemp_ea.pdf

———, "Technical Instructions: Technical Requirements for Design Build," TI 800-03, July 1, 1998a. As of May 8, 2012:
http://www.hnd.usace.army.mil/techinfo/ti/800-03.pdf

———, "Technical Instructions Design Criteria," TI 800-01, July 20, 1998b. As of December 2, 2011:
http://www.hnd.usace.army.mil/techinfo/ti/800-01/ti80001a.htm

———, "Guidance for Firm Fixed-Price Design-Build Construction Contracts," May 14, 2005. As of May 8, 2012:
http://www.hnd.usace.army.mil/chemde/
5-14-2005%20Revised%20D-B%20Clausesweb%20page-Internet-approved.doc

———, "Engineering Guidance Design Manual," March 2008. As of November 28, 2012:
http://www.hnd.usace.army.mil/engr/Documents/
Locked%20Mar%203%202008%20Design%20Manual.pdf

———, "DD Form 1391 Processor System Reference Guide," July 2012. As of October 8, 2012:
www.hnd.usace.army.mil/paxspt/files/RefGuide.pdf

———, "Products," undated(a). As of January 13, 2013:
http://www.hnd.usace.army.mil/paxspt/products.aspx

———, "Products—Economic Analysis Package 4.0.12," undated(b). As of January 13, 2013:
http://www.hnd.usace.army.mil/paxspt/econ/econ.aspx

USACE RFP Wizard, home page, undated. As of January 13, 2013:
http://mrsi.usace.army.mil/rfp/SitePages/Home.aspx

USACE—see U.S. Army Corps of Engineers.

U.S. Department of Defense, "Memorandum of Agreement for Economic Analyses/Life Cycle
Costing for Milcon Design," March 18, 1991. As of December 1, 2011:
http://www.wbdg.org/pdfs/moa.pdf

———, "Programming Cost Estimates for Military Construction," Unified Facilities Criteria, UFC
3-730-01, hosted by the Whole Building Design Guide, June 6, 2011. As of February 9, 2012:
http://www.wbdg.org/ccb/DOD/UFC/ufc_3_730_01.pdf

———, "Unified Facilities Criteria," hosted by the Whole Building Design Guide, 2012a. As of
February 9, 2012:
http://www.wbdg.org/ccb/browse_cat.php?c=4

———, "Unified Facilities Guide Specifications," hosted by the Whole Building Design Guide,
2012b. As of October 8, 2012:
http://www.wbdg.org/ccb/browse_cat.php?c=3

———, Fiscal Year (FY) 2013 Budget Estimates, Military Construction, Family Housing, Defense-Wide,
Justification Data Submitted to Congress, February 2012c. As of January 13, 2013:
http://comptroller.defense.gov/defbudget/fy2013/budget_justification/pdfs/
07_Military_Construction/Military_Construction_Defense-Wide.pdf

———, "Annual Energy Management Report, Fiscal Year 2011," Office of the Deputy
Undersecretary of Defense (Installations and Environment), September 2012d. As of October 8,
2012:
http://www.acq.osd.mil/ie/energy/library/FY.2011.AEMR.PDF

———, "Department of Defense Base Structure Report Fiscal Year 2012 Baseline," Office of
the Deputy Under Secretary of Defense (Installations and Environment), January 7, 2013. As of
January 28, 2013:
http://www.acq.osd.mil/ie/download/bsr/BSR%20Baseline%20FY2012%20Jan072013.pdf

———, "Defense Budget Materials—FY2013," Office of the Under Secretary of Defense
(Comptroller), undated(a). As of May 14, 2012:
http://comptroller.defense.gov/Budget2013.html

———, "Military Construction Appropriations Laws," Pentagon Library, Washington Headquarters
Service, undated(b). As of May 14, 2012:
http://www.whs.mil/library/miltaryconstructionappropriat.htm

U.S. Department of Energy, "The Design-Build Process for the Research Support Facility," 2012a. As
of June 12, 2012:
http://www.nrel.gov/docs/fy12osti/51387.pdf

———, "Building Life-Cycle Cost (BLCC) Programs," last updated December 12, 2012b. As of
January 13, 2013:
http://www1.eere.energy.gov/femp/information/download_blcc.html

U.S. Department of Veterans Affairs, "Code Comparison of IBC 2006 and NFPA 101 2006," May 2007. As of June 12, 2012:
http://www.wbdg.org/ccb/VA/VASTUDIES/codecomparison.pdf

U.S. Green Building Council, "LEED," home page, 2012. As of January 13, 2013:
http://new.usgbc.org/leed

U.S. House of Representatives, "National Defense Authorization Act for Fiscal Year 2011, Report of the Committee on Armed Services, House of Representatives on H.R. 5136," House Report 111-491, accompanying the National Defense Authorization Act for FY 2011, May 21, 2010. As of June 12, 2012:
http://www.gpo.gov/fdsys/pkg/CRPT-111hrpt491/html/CRPT-111hrpt491.htm

U.S. Marine Corps, "Military Construction Planning and Programming Guide," July 13, 2010. As of December 3, 2011:
https://www.hqmc-facilities.org/milcon/guidance/10%20Guidance.pdf

U.S. Navy, "Facilities Projects Instruction," OPNAVINST 11010.20G, September 2, 2010. As of December 3, 2011:
http://doni.daps.dla.mil/Directives/
11000%20Facilities%20and%20Land%20Management%20Ashore/
11-00%20Facilities%20and%20Activities%20Ashore%20Support/11010.20G%20w%20CH-1.pdf

Whole Building Design Guide, "NAVFAC Design-Build Request for Proposal," home page, 2012a. As of January 13, 2013:
http://www.wbdg.org/ndbm/ndbm.php

———, "Parametric Cost Engineering System (PACES)," 2012b. As of January 13, 2013:
http://www.wbdg.org/tools/paces.php?a=1